# *SELL*
## *the*
# *PIG*

**TOTTIE LIMEJUICE**

*I keep six honest serving-men*
*(They taught me all I knew);*
*Their names are What and Why and When*
*And How and Where and Who.*

—Rudyard Kipling
1865-1936

# Foreword

Not another book about a family moving to France! But I can safely guarantee you've never before encountered a family like mine.

There's my brother. A manic-depressive alcoholic. When we each inherited some money from a favourite aunt, I put mine in a high-interest internet bank account. He bought a double decker bus. Like you do.

Then there's Mother, now aged eighty-nine and going through some glorious second childhood where she likes to say "bum" and "bugger" as often as possible.

And there's me. Allegedly the normal one of the family. A middle-aged freelance copywriter with a pretentious collie dog whose name is pronounced Mike but spelt Meic and who has his own email account and blog.

Like so many other Brits, we're heading for France in search of a better life. Where old people are revered, not allowed to starve or become seriously dehydrated, even in hospitals. Where a more relaxed social attitude to drinking might help lessen the need for alcohol abuse. And where dogs are as welcome in restaurants as children.

When I wrote this, we were still playing fox/chicken/corn/ river with the logistics of trying to complete the purchase and organise the move, which involved finding and buying a house in France, and selling two houses and letting a third in the UK. Sell the Pig takes us up to setting foot in France.

If you are looking for a definitive "how to uproot the family and move to France" idiot's guide, this is not the book for you. Much of it is about the background that led us to make the move.

It's not side-splittingly funny and is not intended to be. There are humourous moments, as life is full of them. There are also some sad moments. And possibly some make you angry moments. That's because it's warts and all truth. And that's the way the dice fall.

It's also intensely personal, which some of you may find uncomfortable. But I hope it sets out for you the whys and wherefores of how such a mismatched – some might say dysfunctional – family decided to sever all ties with the UK and move to France.

I've tried to tell things as they happened, without editing or embellishment. But that of itself presents a problem, since one person's account of an event might differ enormously from that of someone else who was there at the same time.

Journalists are always being accused of sensationalism. As a former one myself, I would just say in their defence that if you interview two eyewitnesses to any one event, you will probably get two completely different versions.

The more witnesses you interview, the more versions you are likely to get.

Take a fire, for example. One witness might report flames twenty feet high. Another might say they were two hundred feet high. Which version is likely to sell more newspapers? And at the end of the day, that is part of a journalist's job – to write articles that will make the paper sell.

I've tried to present the facts as I saw them in each incident I write about. Others present at the same time may have seen twenty foot flames to my two hundred foot flames.

If in the reading of this piece you decide I am completely bonkers and ready for a straitjacket, just remember - I'm meant to be the most sane one of the family. Which says a lot about the other two!

*There's so much more to tell. At the risk of sounding presumptuous, there needs to be a sequel. It may well be called Biff the Useless Mention. Which I hope is intriguing enough for you to want to know more.*

# Part One:
# Who

# Mother

They say, as they get old, your parents become your children. That's why, now she's eighty-nine and I'm in my mid fifties, I find myself constantly saying to my mother things like: "Do you need the loo before we go out?" or: "You'll need your coat on, it's cold outside."

And because she's going through some sort of glorious second childhood, I also have to constantly rebuke her for pointing at passing carers and saying: "Look at her big fat bum."

Bum is a word she likes to use frequently. But she still knows enough to recognise it's slightly rude. So she drops it into conversation then collapses in giggles.

Her short-term memory is long gone. She's not quite away with the pixies yet, although gets that way when she's allowed to become dehydrated, an alarmingly frequent occurrence, even in a nursing home or in hospital, or when she has a UTI (urinary tract infection), which also happens all too frequently.

We look through her vast collection of photographs and although she knows the faces of old friends, she mostly can't remember their names. So I prompt her and we play guessing games till she gets it right.

"Who's this?" I'll say, holding up a picture of her best friend.

"Bobby Chops," she'll say at once, which is a favourite phrase she trots out when she can't remember someone's real name.

"Her name is a type of jewel," I tell her. "My birthstone."

"Ruby!" she exclaims triumphantly.

"And who's this?" I say, holding out another picture. "It's the name of another jewel, but it begins with a B."

"Bum!" she cries, and hoots with mirth, which leads to the inevitable: "I'm dying for a wee." And before I can even press the call button, let alone wait the twenty minutes it often takes for someone to respond, she continues: "I'm weeing. Oh well, never mind. God is good, and the Devil's not too bad - to his own."

She's full of these wonderful old phrases and sayings. They make up the majority of her conversation these days. I sometimes hear other people within the nursing home using some of her favourites, and her principal one has become something of her trademark.

"Dear Mother, it's a bugger, sell the pig and buy me out," was allegedly written as a telegram home by some long-forgotten uncle who was not enjoying his first taste of military service. She usually says "Mother, Mother, it's a bugger" and it would be hard to count the number of times a day she says it. It's become her stock phrase when anyone asks how she is.

People are often taken aback to hear what they perceive as a swear-word coming from the lips of a dear old white-haired lady, although in many parts of the country, it's just an everyday word with no particular social taboo. In South Wales, you'll hear it used as almost a term of endearment. People will gaze into prams and say: "Oh love him, there's a bad cold he's got, poor bugger." And in Lancashire, where mother comes from, it's just a word for adverse circumstances.

The fixation with bums is harder to explain. The other day when I visited the nursing home where she is, allegedly, being looked after, I was most surprised to find her apparently absorbed in a rugby match on television, as she has never shown any interest at all in sports, particularly neither team games nor contact sports.

"Rugby, Mother? You?" I asked.

"Yes," she replied, without peeling her gaze away from the heaving flesh of the Australian pack as they went into a scrum. "Look at all those big fat bums."

Mother was born in the part of Lancashire now swallowed up into Merseyside, just before the end of the First World War. The daughter of a master builder, she was one of six children. Well, strictly speaking, there were seven, but little Florrie died very young and is almost never mentioned. In fact, Mother doesn't even know where she is buried, a curious fact, since visiting the graves of various long-dead family members was always a tradition on anniversaries.

Mother sometimes says her mother blamed her father for killing Florrie. I don't imagine she's hinting at some real child murder. I think rather, from piecing together snippets of what she has said over the years, that probably Granny felt little Florrie was seriously ill and wanted Grandpa to go for the doctor but he either couldn't or wouldn't. So Florrie died. But those may be two hundred foot flames, not twenty.

I never knew my Grandpa James, he died before I was born, of some sort of abdominal torsion. I do know that this made Mother paranoid on the subject of our bowel habits and whether or not we had "been" each day, throughout our childhood.

Mother was in the middle of the children, if you can have a middle of six – I have never been famous for my arithmetic. There was Tom, Ethel, Harold, my mother Nell, Doris, and John. Little Florrie was one of the early ones but as her brief life and sudden death were always shrouded in mystery, I'm still unsure where she fitted in.

Tom was the smiler. Ethel, who never married, was the home-maker, who cooked and cleaned and looked after her younger siblings. Harold was the quiet and painfully shy one who never left home, apart from wartime service when he saw action on the Anzio beach-head as an infantry man. Apparently he lost his service boots in the mud and developed such bad trench foot the problems stayed with him for the rest of his life.

Mother was a real looker, with beautiful blonde hair so long she could sit on it, who surprisingly didn't marry until she was thirty. Doris was the dizzy blonde who made the good marriage. And John was always the baby of the family, even when he pre-deceased all three of his sisters.

Mother certainly had her share of admirers. In fact she went out with the man Doris went on to marry, before her younger sister did. I have no idea why she waited so long nor eventually made the choice she did.

Recently, when age and dementia have removed inhibitions, Mother has taken to looking wistfully at her wedding photographs and saying: "That was the day. I wonder if I did the right thing?". A sentiment I have certainly shared throughout most of my life.

Father was a journalist, who rose to the dizzy heights of editing the Alderley, Wilmslow and Knutsford Advertiser local weekly newspaper in Cheshire, long before the invasion of Alderley Edge by the likes of footballers with obscene wealth. Although there was quite a stir in his day when the legendary footballer George Best had the most disgusting architect-designed modern house built in neighbouring Bramhall.

Never remotely ambitious, father managed somehow to be made President of the Guild of British Newspaper Editors, which brought a heady whirl of social engagements for him and Mother, including the inevitable Royal Garden Party, at Buckingham Palace.

*Mother and Father made a handsome couple at the many social engagements they had to attend.*

He was always known, within the family, as the AP (Aged Parent). In a family where terms of endearment were rare, nicknames became the norm. He, rather unkindly, referred to my brother as Gutrot because of his habit of reacting to any kind of stress, particularly travel, since the AP's driving was fairly horrendous, by projectile vomiting.

I was dubbed Clara Bow-legs by my brother, since riding was my passion. My escape from the madhouse which was home was to go up to the local riding stables, usually at about 6am and stay there as long as possible, often till late into the evening.

To this day, Mother doesn't realise that I also spent a lot of what should have been school time up at the stables, which may explain why, despite allegedly above average intelligence, I never excelled academically.

The AP's mother came from Luxembourg. She arrived in England as a young girl, to work as a children's nurse, knowing very few words of English. She was the daughter of a farmer, and what led her to make such a monumental journey, for that period in history, has been lost in the mists of time. She was extremely adept at languages, like most natives of such a very small country, and once she quickly mastered English, she spoke six, including Esperanto.

The AP liked to bore for Britain on the subject of his mixed race. Visitors to our home would be plied with the lethal Luxembourg fire-water called Quetsch, distilled from plums, and if that wasn't enough to make their eyes glaze over, being forced to listen to the AP going on about his maternal homeland for several hours certainly was.

He also made an art form of embarrassing his children. A father's prerogative, many would say. But I can remember the cringing feeling when he was telling yet another hapless visitor about the processions through the streets of Echternach, where his aunt lived, to mark the feast of St Willibrord. Townsfolk would hold handkerchiefs and perform a dance as they processed. And how I wished the ground could have swallowed me up when the AP whipped out his handkerchief, passed one end to me and began skipping and hopping his way round the sitting room chanting: "Heilige Willibrord".

Why Mother married him in the first place is enough of a mystery. What possessed her to remain with him for more than forty years is unfathomable. In their way, I suppose, they were happy. But when he died before her, of cancer of the pancreas, at home in bed, with me standing beside him, she was hardly bowled over by grief. In fact, the very same day, she, my brother and I all went out for tea.

Mother had been a stay at home wife and mother until I started secondary school. My brother and I both attended the same primary school, St John's C of E Primary, which was housed in the church and its vestry. Mother would walk with us the mile or so to school until we were both deemed old enough to go by ourselves.

My brother was always the clingy one, I the independent one. When Mother left us at the school gates, he would always say: "Come for me, mum," while I would say equally emphatically: "Don't come for me, mum."

When I started at Stockport High School for girls at age eleven, Mother announced that she intended to go out to work. She had found herself a position, through friends of friends, as the manageress of a wallpaper and paint shop in a nearby town.

Mother was always very talented at interior décor. It became a family joke that our normal greeting, as we came through the door at the end of the day, was not so much: "Hello, have you had a nice day?" but rather: "Mind the paint!"

She was perpetually painting something, hanging new wallpaper somewhere, or making new curtains for one room or another. She even re-enamelled the bath on one memorable occasion.

Meg, my best friend from school days, still talks fondly about the first time she came to stay with me. In preparing the guest room for her, my mother had gone one better than a quick spring clean and had redecorated it from floor to ceiling.

So the decorating shop was absolutely perfect for her and she loved every minute of working there. It also gave her a little bit of financial independence. I'm not entirely sure whether or not there was also a little bit of dalliance going on there, too.

My Saturdays were usually all spent up at the local riding school. I was paid absolute peanuts to muck out, groom, tack up, take rides out, give lessons and all manner of other things, for very long hours. But the bonus was I got the chance to ride, for free. And those of you who have ever been truly, madly, deeply in love with horses, will know that it is an addiction for which you will do absolutely anything.

Mother insisted sometimes that I should instead go and help her out at the shop, for which I received almost twice as much money. But I hated it. You can take the girl out of the stables but you can't take the stables out of the girl.

The friend of a friend who owned the shop would always visit to see how the day had gone, compare notes with my mother and pay me my dues out of the petty cash. He was always impeccably polite and called my mother correctly by her married status and surname.

I wasn't there every week, a lot of the time I refused point blank to go. But there was one occasion when I was there but had gone into the store cupboard under the stairs in search of a particular washable vinyl bathroom wallpaper someone had ordered.

So when Colin came into the shop he couldn't see me and obviously didn't know I was there, since he addressed Mother by her first name and in a much more affectionate tone than I had heard from him before. But I truly don't know if this was just coincidence.

My father's job as a newspaper editor came with a heavy social engagement schedule. There were endless civic receptions, cheese and wine parties, film premiers and other such delights to attend, for which Mother would put on her finest gowns. And they did make a handsome couple, it has to be said.

Father was also a food critic, writing restaurant reviews for his, and other, newspapers. He and Mother would go to a restaurant, by arrangement, rather than a spot visit, choose from the menu, hopefully enjoy the food, and the AP would then write one of his long, rambling reviews, since his writing style was definitely flowery.

All that free dining nearly got Mother and me into hot water some years later, when she was staying with me at my home in Wales. She'd promised to take me out to lunch. I was working as a local newspaper reporter and covering magistrates' court sessions, so every other Friday, when the bench was sitting in the town, I would eat at Llandeilo's Cawdor Hotel, which did a very fine lunch.

I left Mother to browse the small town while I covered the morning court session, and we arranged to meet in their Buttery Bar at lunch time, her treat.

We enjoyed a very pleasant lunch, as did the entire bench of magistrates, the clerk of the court, the senior prosecuting police officer (this being long before the days of the Crown Prosecution Service) and all the various solicitors and occasional barrister appearing for prosecution and defence alike, who all used to eat there.

When we'd finished eating, Mother simply picked up her coat and started to leave. I stage whispered to her that we hadn't yet had the bill, which she had promised to pay.

In a voice the entire assembled judiciary could hear, she said: "Pay? Oh no, we never pay."

Ground opening up and swallowing me moment again.

Mother had always enjoyed the various trips abroad she had made. She had, of course, visited father's family in Luxembourg on many occasions, and spent her honeymoon there. And during the 1980s, when I lived in Germany for four years, she enjoyed her trips out there to visit me.

She'd frequently visited my brother in the time he spent living and working in Brussels.

She also liked to come and stay at my cottage in Lincolnshire or at my brother's house in South Wales. But as she got older and started to get more confused, we were advised that these trips were no longer helpful to her, as the change from her daily routine was too unsettling.

Mother lived in a medium sized semi-detached house in what had always been considered a posh part of Stockport. She'd lived in the house since 1954 and continued to live there alone after my father died in 1988.

She had always been quite capable of managing on her own. We hoped she would continue to do so for a long time. Unfortunately, life doesn't always work out as one would wish.

# Brother

You can choose your friends but you can't chose your family, they say. I have one brother, to whom I refer, unknown to him, as the Idiot Brother or IB. Why do I call him an idiot? It's certainly not for want of intellect, since his intelligence is almost frightening.

He gets by adeptly in about four European languages including Russian, used to play piano very well by ear, although latterly that's gone by the wayside, sings opera tolerably well, is perpetually part-way through a Master's Degree in European Law, is skilled in woodwork, building crafts, electronics and goodness knows what other practical crafts. Yet he seems to inhabit a strange, alien planet, which I call Planet IB, which bears only a passing resemblance to life as we know it, Jim.

I try to make sisterly allowances. After all, nobody joins a queue and says please make me an alcoholic, where do I sign up? Oh, and by the way, if you could also throw in bi-polar disorder and chronic depression, that would be tickety-boo.

But I find it incredibly hard to comprehend why someone who could always do my maths homework in his sleep while I couldn't even understand the questions, cannot work out that if six bottles of wine and one of Vermouth disappear in twenty-four hours inside a house in which you are the only occupant, you must, by definition, be drunk.

And that it's probably, therefore, not a very clever idea to be up a wobbling, unsecured ladder without a safety harness, attempting to cut down a very large twisted willow tree. With an electric circular saw. With no safety guard. In a high wind. And lashing rain. With no retaining ropes in place to direct any falling timber away from the triple-wall polycarbonate roof of the outbuilding just below it.

That's just one example of his behaviour which I produce as evidence for my opinion. My particular favourite centres on when he and I each received a little money when Auntie Ethel, of whom I was particularly fond, died. Being of a prudent nature, I carefully put my money into a high interest internet bank account, where it remains to this day. The IB bought a Leyland Routemaster double-decker bus. Like you do.

In today's climate, no doubt a school psychologist would have stuck a label on him, almost certainly something on the autistic spectrum. Because although alcoholism was clearly not a factor in his early years, certainly his behaviour, even as a toddler, could not have been labelled as "normal."

Lots of small children, of course, have imaginary companions. Mine was a cowboy called Rocky and it certainly taxed my poor mother's imagination to come up with appeasements when I refused to wear "girlie" clothes on the grounds they were not worn in Rocky's Land. But public transport frequently had to be held up to wait for the IB's troupe of imaginary kittens. And to hear him give his version of any event we'd both attended would put Walter Mitty to shame.

Then there were the terrible rages. As a very small toddler he would bang his head repeatedly against the sides of his cot in such fury that it later transpired he had broken his nose, probably several times over, in the process. And when taken reluctantly for new shoes one day, much to my mother's mortification, he pelted the poor unfortunate sales assistant with the dolly mixtures which had been bought in the forlorn hope of bribing or pacifying him into acceptable behaviour.

Is it nature or nurture which determines how someone will turn out? I believe the jury is still out on the definitive answer. But in the IB's case, his formative years cannot have been helped by a father who would repeat several times a day, like a mantra: "The lad's a fool", to anyone who would listen, and always within earshot of my brother.

And if it's nature, it can't have helped that our maternal grandfather, whom I never met, was certainly a heavy drinker, if not an alcoholic. Nor that at least two of the more distant Luxembourg cousins committed suicide as young men and another less distant attempted it on more than one occasion, through depression.

What I remember most about growing up with my brother was him being sick. At our very small junior school, every Monday morning was diary day, when we all had to write about what we did at the weekend.

Our main family activity was hiking in the Peak District or Derbyshire Dales. The AP would don one of the ludicrous striped woollen bobble caps he affected, Mother would pack hard boiled eggs and Jacob's Club biscuits (there must have been other food, but those are the things I remember best) and we'd head off for a family ramble. And as ever, the IB would punctuate the journey there and back with projectile vomiting.

So my Monday morning diary would read: "We went to Pott Shrigley and my brother was sick." "We went to Monsal Dale and my brother was sick." "We went to Kinder Scout and my brother was sick." I'm sure the teacher (there was only one, the school was so small) thought I was making it all up.

There was one memorable occasion when he was still being sick when we got back to the house, and managed to throw up on my rose bush – I was keen on gardening from a tender age. I'm not sure I ever fully forgave him for that act of treachery.

To some measure, although entirely unintentionally, I consider myself in some small part to blame for the projectile vomiting. My brother was four years old when I was born, and to read his early baby book, he seems to have had the undivided attention of both our parents until that moment.

*Quintessential 1960s middle class family. Mother, Father, Brother and Me, with my brother's African godfather.*

Then his life was turned completely upside down by the arrival of a baby sister. I know sibling rivalry is fairly common in most families. But fate added an extra touch in our case.

When I was not yet a year old, I developed very severe whooping cough. My parents always told me it was so bad I would frequently cough and whoop until I was sick and then passed out.

They also told me, although this might have been more two hundred foot flames, that they were told that I might not survive.

Unsurprisingly, my illness took up a lot of their time and attention and I imagine it may well have caused my brother, a very sensitive child, to feel left out. And to notice that children being sick got the most attention.

I'm not exactly sure when my brother started drinking to any degree. It's surprisingly hard to notice such things – there is alcoholism in many families with even close family members being blissfully unaware of the extent of the problem. When I was a young journalist, a ten vodka lunch was fairly routine, and the AP was very fond of a drink, including some utterly disgusting home brewed rotgut which would have done a good job of treating a garden fence.

I don't think I truly realised the extent of my brother's problem until all bridges were burnt, I had moved into his house and let my own, and we were all systems go for the great adventure, the move to France.

He had always been a bit, well, different, for want of a better word. He never made friends easily and had even more difficulty in keeping them. My friendships go back for years - I'm still friends with Meg from 1963!

My brother also had a rather annoying habit of feeding off my friends all the time. He'd latch on to them and try to make them his own. It began in school-days, when he started dating friends I brought back to the house. But that's a fairly normal thing – after all I went out with Meg's brother for a time and am still in contact with him now.

Two of the things about him that tend to make friends run for the hills are that he loves to talk about himself, especially his latest ailments, real or imaginary. And whilst he can't wait to come round and tell you all about the bad days and bad luck he's been having, you seldom get to share the good bits. When he's feeling on form, he takes himself off and treats himself somewhere, to a meal out and perhaps a night in an hotel, without extending the invitation to those who have helped him through the bad times.

But for all his faults, he has always had an amazing sense of humour and been fond of very elaborate and well thought out practical jokes. He worked for a time for the European Commission in Brussels. He would spend time producing very official looking directives, in correct, formal French, which would send everyone into a flat spin when they were circulated.

One stated that The Republic of Ireland had decided to fall in line with motoring rules within the other member states by converting to driving on the right hand side of the road. At all border crossings into Northern Ireland, there would therefore be special cross-over stations where vehicles would change from driving on the left in the north to driving on the right in the republic.

Another stated that the use of official languages within the commission's buildings in Brussels was too discriminatory, so that in future a mixture of languages would be spoken on different days of the week. But they were paired up into minority languages, so that the chances of many people knowing either of the appointed languages for the day would be slim. For example, Monday would be Welsh and Portuguese, Tuesday, Greek and Danish, and so on.

He'd phone people up, speaking with a thick foreign accent and claiming to be some extraordinary person or other and could string them along for ages. Other friends of mine would get mail to their address in the name of someone they'd never heard of which, when examined closely, would be a very clever play on words.

But somewhere along the way, the drink took over. And drink, being a depressive substance itself, is a very dangerous thing for someone who suffers from depression. It's also highly addictive, as much as any drug.

So much fuss is made about cannabis. But compared to the havoc wreaked on so many lives by alcohol, it must surely pale into insignificance. I have many friends who smoke a little blow and get up to nothing more serious than serial giggling. But the transformation of personality which alcohol can cause is something else entirely.

I had once, briefly, shared living space with my brother. I moved back to the UK in 1984, after living in Germany for four years, and started running an equestrian centre. Around the same time, my brother's marriage broke up and he was going through a very bad patch, so he came to live at the riding centre and helped with some jobs around the place, like putting in a fitted kitchen. I have no memory of excessive drinking then. But sometime after that, he started on the slippery downward slope of using a bottle as a place of refuge.

# Meic

If you don't like dogs, this is the part you need to skip. But since dogs occupy such a big place in my life, and since Meic did in particular, it's only fair I write a bit about him. And you'll note that his chapter comes before mine, which should help you to place in context his importance in my life.

I've lived alone for a long time, since about the mid 1980s. First through circumstance then later on through choice. But there's always been at least one dog around, and the current one at the time of writing this and embarking on the adventure was Meic.

For those of you who hate reading things you don't know how to pronounce, his name is pronounced Mike and is a sort-of pseudo Welsh spelling just for fun, although he was always known as Mikey.

Meic was a very well bred sheepdog from top working lines. His mother was an international sheepdog trials champion. With the kind of bad luck that sometimes dogs me (please excuse the pun) I got the one dog in the litter to suffer from psycho-motor seizures, a form of epilepsy.

He was my best friend, my confidant, my constant companion. At the age of eight, some time before the decision for us all to uproot and move to France, he was diagnosed with a serious heart condition and given a prognosis of one to two years.

For a long time I'd had a hankering desire to go and settle in France. Being not entirely English left me with not quite the same attachment to the British Isles as other Brits, although born and raised there. Plus numerically speaking, I have far more relatives on the continent, since Granny came from quite a large family.

So when the time came to start thinking seriously about making the move to France, Meic was a major consideration for me. He'd already outlived his gloomy prognosis by nearly three years. But was it really sensible to up sticks with a dog in his teens, with a serious heart condition, and move him a thousand miles away to a different country?

I'd always had such good vets, and although the lovely Archie in Market Rasen was wrong in his prognosis, he was wrong in the best possible way. Meic was still going strong years after his initial diagnosis and still enjoying playing with his squeaky toys.

I'm sure there are those amongst you, if you've read thus far, who will be thinking why not just put him to sleep and move and get a new dog once installed in France? Trouble is, I'm a bit of a softie with my dogs and always apply the Squeaky Toy Rule – as long as a dog is still quite happy to play with a favourite toy, there's too much life there to extinguish, in my humble opinion.

So with all Meic's problems to take into account – not least of which was the consideration of expensive heart and arthritis medications to buy, since he'd reached the cut-off age on his insurance – I'd always firmly said that any move to France would be AM – After Meic.

*Meic, my best friend, constant companion and confidant - quite simply, my boy.*

The great thing about Meic was that he was very much a people dog – he got on with everyone and everyone got on with him, even those who didn't like dogs or were afraid of them. He was big for a collie – I was often asked if he was a cross-bred, usually a Bernese mountain dog cross – but he was pure collie and pure softie through and through.

He'd got me through a lot of tough times, changes of job, changes of home, uprooting from one place to go to another one I didn't know. So it was unthinkable for me not to take him with me.

Equally importantly, Mother loved him and he was so sweet and gentle with her. He was a regular visitor to the various homes she lived in, where he was equally popular with staff and residents alike.

At the very nice home in St Helens, Mother's home town, where she was happy and well looked after, several of the old ladies in residence would claim him as "their" dog whenever he visited. One would say: "Eeeeh, it's our Sandy. Hello our Sandy," and Meic would obligingly thump his tail softly and lick a hand and be Sandy for a while.

Then it would be: "Eeeeeh, it's our Bobby", from another old lady, and he'd repeat the process, being Bobby for a few minutes.

Mother always called him Baby for some reason, although at nearly thirty kilogrammes, there was nothing particularly baby-ish about him.

And yes, translation note for those of you not from "oop north", in parts of Lancashire they do indeed say "eeeeeh", though I've never heard it followed by "bah gum", except ironically. And everyone is always "our", pronounced ow-ur with two distinct syllables.

In fact as Mother got more and more befuddled and was living permanently in care or nursing homes, Meic always got much more of a welcome from her than I did. He was a very intelligent dog; if he could have mastered driving I could quite happily have sent him by himself and stayed at home without needing to visit.

I'd heard how the French were equally, if not more so, a nation of dog lovers as the British. In fact, apparently nearly thirty per cent of households in France own a dog. So I was confident that Meic would land on his paws, as usual, and be perfectly happy in his new home country.

Another major concern was for heart worm, which occurs in parts of France, not a risk worth taking with an older dog with a heart condition. But we were now into the era of passports for pets so I knew I could fairly easily get him back to the UK if it became necessary, without the stress and expense of quarantine kennels, as I'd previously had to do with another collie when returning to the UK after four years of living in Germany.

So one way or another, if I was headed for France earlier than intended, Meic was definitely coming with me.

I hadn't exactly intended to get Meic. When I'd left my riding centre in Wales, in the early nineties, to move to Dorset, I had a small black collie cross named Mady. She came from a rescue centre, where she was called Mandy, but she was so definitely not a Mandy, I just dropped the N and she became Mady. It was in part a nod to the incredibly talented Maddy Prior, of Steeleye Span.

She was very happy as an only dog. She was a very easy and biddable dog, though inclined to be a little bit bossy with other dogs. She did on one occasion up-end my friend's lovely Staffie, Camilla, whilst giving away a huge amount of weight in the contest. That's how tough and determined she was.

I'd kept in touch with old friends in Wales when I left there to move to Dorset, and some of them were kind enough to provide work experience placements for the learning disabled students I was responsible for whilst working there. So I would visit them whenever I went down to check up on the students' progress.

One friend, who had been my riding instructor when I was living there, bred working sheepdogs, and was a frequent competitor with them in trials. I knew she had a couple of pups left from the latest litter off her very good trialling bitch Daz and a big, heavy set dog, Marc, whom I'd known from a puppy.

I wasn't in the market for another dog. There was no danger at all of my wanting one when Anna-Lou showed me the remaining two puppies. But then I saw Meic. Or Mott, as he was called at that time. And something cracked. To Mady's intense disgust, she found herself sharing the back of the car on the way home with a squeaking, peeing, puking puppy who had not had much experience of car travel.

And so Meic burst into our lives. He was by no stretch of the imagination a puppy farm dog, he was very well bred, from a very good home, well socialised with other dogs. But he was kennel bred and raised and took a little bit of time to learn about house training.

He was only about nine months old when he started with the first of his seizures. I just thought he was an incredibly disobedient dog as he sometimes seemed to completely ignore me. It later transpired that he was suffering petit mal absences, another form of epilepsy.

The medication he was put on to control his seizures had the rare, but not unheard of, side-effect of making him hyperactive, rather than zombie-like as is usually the case. And as most collies are pretty hyper to begin with, it was lethal.

His favourite trick when high on medication was to take himself off upstairs then launch himself down the steep staircase in an attempt to build up enough steam to be able to swing round the corner into the living room and then do a wall of death right round the room without setting paw to floor. He would boing from settee to window sill to table to mantelpiece with astonishing agility and ease, in a way which would put many a cat to shame.

I decided we could do without the side-effects and stopped the medication, preferring just to manage the seizures as and when they occurred. Especially as the medication was extremely liver-unfriendly and necessitated him having frequent blood tests to check that things were as they should be.

Meic was my seventh dog and fourth collie. I had always wanted a dog but was never allowed to have one as a child. We had a succession of cats in the family. One in particular I remember well, a grey tabby called, innocuously, Topsy.

Killer or Satan or Hellcat might have been more appropriate. She was a foul-tempered creature who would lie in wait on the stairs to leap on the legs and feet of any mere mortal foolish enough to try to pass her. She would pounce, grab firm hold of the leg with her front feet, sink her dear little fangs deep into the flesh then commence that very effective disembowelling action cats do with their strong back legs. Truly a delight.

As soon as I had a wage coming in and the means to afford one, I got my first dog. Perro, Pez to his friends, or to give him his full title, Velindre Gorsefield Lobo, was a big German Shepherd Dog, incredibly handsome, black and gold, and so striking people would often stop me in the street to ask about him. It was like going out with a film star.

I got him when he was just nine months old, and convinced Mother that what I was about to bring home was still just a puppy and would be no trouble at all. Even at that age he was a very big dog – he grew into a seven stone hulk of a dog. But once he'd pinned Mother up against her Welsh dresser and was covering her with big sloppy kisses, she couldn't really say no.

I could go anywhere at any time of the day or night with that dog by my side and heaven help anyone who even looked at me in an aggressive way. He was as sweet as anything with friends and family, but heaven help any stranger who tried to get too close to me without his permission.

Meic was a different character altogether. For a big, lively dog, he was very good with people and quite happy with visitors. When Mother was staying with us, he would climb onto the settee beside her – dogs in my home are allowed to go anywhere I go – and lay his head gently on her lap while she watched television.

I hadn't had a dogless day since 1970 and I certainly wasn't going to contemplate having the first of them in a new home in a new country. Against all the odds, I became more and more determined that when plans for a move to France were taking shape, Meic should be a part of them.

After all, we were planning, against what most other people said was sensible or feasible, to uproot a nearly ninety-year-old mother with various heart conditions and take her to live abroad. So what was the difference between her and a collie who was around ninety in equivalent human years and also had a heart condition?

# Me

So now it's time to tell you a little bit about me. And I'm sure most of you will want to know, who the heck is Tottie Limejuice?

She's an invention of my Auntie Ethel. You remember her, the unmarried home maker. Although, to be fair, in her day she had been a fashion buyer for a big department store in St Helens, so not quite the stay at home mouse.

Auntie had a wonderful turn of phrase and was always coming up with weird and wonderful words which we were not sure existed. The AP, as a newspaper editor, liked to be very superior and scoff at some of them. But he was wrong about tracklements, which he always claimed she made up.

As Auntie got older, she too became a bit confused and, as is often the case with dementia, she began to be suspicious of those around her. She became particularly so of her brother-in-law, who was married to her younger sister, Doris. It was largely resentment. He was a judge and solicitor and took care of all the family's personal and financial affairs. And I think it stuck in her craw to have him controlling her purse strings, although it was for her own good.

Auntie Ethel was a very nice favourite auntie. She made all her own clothes, and her own hats, but was never especially glamorous. So it was amusing in a sad sort of way that in later years she started to accuse younger sister Doris, who really was the glamorous one, with a shoe collection to rival Imelda Marcos, of stealing her clothes and especially her rather large home-made drawers.

She would say: "She comes up here, taking my things and swanning round like Tottie Limejuice." I adopted it as a pen name and it rather stuck. To many of my friends now I am, and always will be, Tottie or Tots.

But what is the real me? If it were not for the fact that I inherited my father's nose and my mother's feet (thanks for the bunions, Mother) I would suspect I was a changeling, as I am so unlike the rest of my family. In particular I have virtually nothing, other than genes, in common with my brother. He is cat, I am dog. He is city, I am country. He is extravagance, I am thrift. You get the general picture.

I think the genes I inherited skipped a generation because I'm most like my Luxembourg granny. She was a farmer's daughter who used to love to go and collect her townie cousins and drive them back rather too fast in the carriage with her favourite horse. When I took up carriage driving I took delight in taking out a rather obnoxious boss and scaring her witless by driving slightly too fast.

I would have liked to have been a vet but I'm not intelligent enough. I can't do maths, so I struggle with many sciences. So I ended up becoming a journalist, despite being determined not to follow my father into his profession.

I also kept up my interest in horses, got a few qualifications with them and did a bit of teaching and lecturing in the subject. I've owned and run one equestrian centre and managed another.

I've done all sorts of jobs to earn a crust – I'm not proud – including being a chugger for the Wildlife Trusts. A charity mugger, that is. You know, the annoying folk lurking outside super-markets who pounce on you just as you're about to leave, causing you to drop your bag of sprouts all over the foyer.

They're so annoying that I suppose they deserve some of the strange replies they get to their cheery: "Can I interest you in the Wildlife Trust?" I think my personal favourite remains: "No, but my husband does it with birds." And no, I'm not sure I've quite worked that one out either.

Most recently I've made a living of sorts as a freelance copy-writer. Don't worry, most people don't know what one of those is, either. We're the equally annoying folk behind the mail order catalogues, brochures, flyers, emails etc which coerce you into buying things because their honeyed words make you believe you just can't live without them.

I sometimes feel it's a rather silly job for a grown-up as I sit at my computer scratching my head to come up with wince-mak-ing puns and corny headlines because the client is determined to be "quirky". But most of the time I love it.

It's a crazy job, with often impossible deadlines, and it's a scary position to be in as one gets older. There are so many eager young things snapping at your heels as you struggle with the daily learning curves of keeping up with ever-evolving things like social media and all the gadgetry that goes with it.

The big advantage, though, is it's something that can be done remotely, from anywhere with a broadband internet connection. Especially as I'm fortunate and privileged to work with a col-league who is also a good friend and does all the flesh-pressing and schmoozing of the clients, leaving me to tap away at the keyboard behind the scenes.

Just as well really, as when I'm sitting here writing about the latest fashions, I'm usually, depending on the season, wearing several fleeces, fleece lined trousers and ski socks, or shorts and an ancient washed-out polo shirt.

When I'm not at the keyboard, I like to be outside, walking with a dog or two, camping, in all weathers including snow, gardening, or just reading a book outdoors. I can read a map, I don't have a sat nav and get almost as much pleasure from getting the maps out to plan my next camping trip as actually going on it.

For those who set truck by such things, I'm a Leo, with many typical characteristics. And, according to the Chinese, I'm also a Dragon, some would say appropriately. I make a good friend but a very bad enemy. I'm ferociously independent and prefer a small circle of very close friends to a large one of superficial friendships. That's why it's never been a problem for me, if things don't work out in one place, to pick myself up by the bootlaces and move somewhere else to try again.

And another typical Leo trait – I'm a real cock-eyed optimist. People think being an optimist is good, but it isn't really. If you're a pessimist, your life is full of pleasant surprises as things often turn out to be not as bad as you fear. We rose-tinted optimists experience a lot of disappointments in life as our expectations are often unrealistically high.

All of which is worth bearing in mind as you hopefully continue to plod through this saga.

It may help to explain some decisions I have made which might otherwise seem completely barmy. Perhaps they have been barmy, but it's a barminess born out of that over-developed optimism.

What's that? We want to know more about me? In more detail? Oh, all right then. But I'm not telling you everything.

I was born in Nantwich, the posh end of Cheshire. My father was at that time the editor and district manager of the local newspaper. Whilst we lived there, according to my mother, my brother spoke with the long, posh "a" sound typical of the area. I was still too young to speak with any accent. He would go into the garden to make sand "caaahstles".

After a short time, we moved up to Preston, when my father transferred to the Lancashire Evening Post. Within a very short time, my brother had adopted the very short, flat "a" sound of that area and would play at making sand "casstles".

I think I was about two when we moved again to Offerton, the refined end of Stockport, when my father joined the Stockport Advertiser. And there we stayed, as when he transferred to the Wilmslow Advertiser, there was no way his modest salary would fund a house there, even before the arrival of the footballers.

Whilst at junior school, I was an enthusiastic brownie in the First Offerton pack and rose to the heady rank of fairy sixer. I passed all my various tests to win my Golden Hand, which entitled me to "fly up" to Guides. And in those days passing was no mean feat.

Some of the tests were quite tricky. I remember having to go round to the District Commissioner's house to lay and light her open fire. And I remember the sadistic examiner we had for semaphore, who thought a long-winded message about penguins in the zoological gardens was a fair test of the semaphore skills of a ten-year-old.

I quite enjoyed junior school, most of the time. It was very small, I think there were probably no more than fifty pupils in total over junior and infants. There was one teacher for each of the two complete sections. The juniors sat in rows according to age, down the nave of the church, the infants had little desks, all together in the vestry.

The headteacher would start on the first row by age, teach them something then leave them to get on with it while she moved onto the next row. And so on. She ruled with a rod of iron – literally. She had a long steel rule and a garden cane with which any boy who stepped out of line was soundly thrashed. Girls got their hands or legs smacked, according to how heinous was their crime.

Things were very primitive, with toilets outside in the school yard and an extremely temperamental coke-fired boiler down in the cellar, tended by a handyman, which gave off such foul-smelling fumes it's a wonder any of us lived to tell the tale. When we reached the top class we took on extra responsibilities, like carting out buckets to flush the toilets which regularly froze up.

Once a week the Mothers' Union would take over the vestry after the infants had gone home, and as my mother was a member, I would go and join them to wait for her and walk home with her. My abiding memory is of a bottled gas fire which always smelled, and buttered Scotch pancakes with tea, although I'm sure there must have been other delicacies.

In those heady days before 'Elf and Safety went completely mad and risk assessments had to be done on anything and everything from colouring pencils upwards, we used to go on nature walks. And every year, it being a C of E school, we went on a school trip on Ascension Day, with the vicar and his spinster sister, who was his housekeeper.

The vicar was very interested in, and knowledgeable on, wild flowers, and used to love using the names of some of them as pseudo swear words. "Stinking hellebore!" he would exclaim, when things went wrong. Or "Bloody cranesbill!"

I also sang in the very tiny school choir, and in those days, the whole school squashed together into one room once a week to listen to Singing Together, with William Appleby. We sang all sorts of wonderful old folk songs like "The Lincolnshire Poacher" and "The Keeper did a-Hunting Go."

I once met someone of my age, from Sunderland, who had a theory that belting out "Jackie Boy! Massster! Sing ye well? Very well. Hey down, ho down, derry-derry-down", at very high volume, reduced aggression in a class of young boys who might otherwise have been a real handful. He may well have been right. I know everyone seemed to enjoy those broadcasts and settled down to work better after them.

My brother was at the same primary school and I can remember, when I was still in the infants and he in juniors, how proud I was on Singing Together days to be allowed to go and squash up onto the seat between him and his school friend as there were not enough chairs for all the infants as well as the juniors.

I didn't like "big" school, where I went after passing my eleven plus. It wasn't very big, only about 400 pupils, but seemed enormous and impersonal after coming from such a small school. I also felt, from the very start, that I was not in control of my destiny. I was harbouring an admittedly unrealistic notion of being a vet. But in the modern world of education, our German science teacher, Miss Hock, would not have been allowed to say scornfully and dismissively: "You will never be a vet", and leave it at that.

I quite fancied modern languages, coming from a family of polyglots. In second year (as it was called then - no idea what that equates to in modern parlance) we had to choose between Latin and German. I opted for German and went along to the first lesson with Miss Stansfield. I'd already thoroughly enjoyed listening to her reading aloud to us Der Erlkönig, one day as a special end of term treat. Even though I didn't understand a word, she made it sound so exciting.

I was just settling down for my first ever German lesson when the deputy head, Miss Wilkinson, who also taught Latin and Greek, marched into the classroom and frog-marched me out with her and into her Latin class. I, I was told, would be doing Latin, not German. Of course I was not asked if that was what I wanted.

With the benefit of hindsight, though, I am pleased I was made to do Latin. I was quite good at it, getting honours in most of my exams, and found it an invaluable base for other languages, and a great help with learning English grammar.

Because I could string two notes together, I was press-ganged into the school choir, with rehearsals two lunch-times a week, and because I took up the violin, but only to avoid having to play lacrosse, which I hated, as violin lessons clashed with lacrosse practice, I was also drafted into the school orchestra, with rehearsals after school two nights a week. What with all that and working Saturdays, some evenings and holidays up at the riding school, I took the decision not to join the girl guides, although their outdoor activities were right up my street.

Meg was a member of her local guide group and whenever I stayed with her, I went along as a sort of honorary member. I remember lots of bonfires and making dampers which, if you are not familiar with them, are a fairly disgusting basic dough mixture made from flour, water, a multitude of no doubt life-threatening microbes and plenty of dirt, threaded onto a stick probably cut from a highly poisonous shrub or tree, and held perilously close to the flames till they had enough carcinogenic carbonisation to be consumed. How did my generation ever live as long as we have?

Above all, I was, and always have been, bolshie. Ask me to do something for you, and if it's remotely within my power, I will do it willingly. Tell me I have to do something and I'll probably refuse point blank. It's an attitude that has got me into a lot of trouble in life, particularly at school.

Those were the days when schools had the power to clap pupils into detention for the least little thing. And did. Detention at our school involved reporting to a particular room on the mezzanine floor at ten past four, as everyone else was leaving, and sitting there for half an hour writing lines or whatever else one had been set by the teacher who'd sentenced you.

Detention happened twice a week and I was always in it. On the very rare occasions when I wasn't and arrived home early, my mother was always surprised to see me. Some of the nicer and more gullible teachers were easy to dupe. There was a flat roof outside the detention room, so we would all climb out of the window onto the roof and duck down.

The duty teacher would come along, find the room empty, wait around for a few moments then go. We'd all then climb back in, sit innocently at desks for a few minutes then go home and swear blind the next day we had reported for detention as ordered but that no teacher had come along to take the register.

I've always written, all my life. I'd always have a scribbled diary, or story, on the go. I wrote for, and later edited, a national magazine for sixth formers, and did some articles and reviews for my father's paper on occasion.

My best friend Meg and I were also passionate about westerns. Her next door neighbour was an elderly lady who lived alone and had one of the first colour televisions we'd seen. She was more than happy for us to go round to watch our current favourite, The High Chaparral, each week.

Meg and I both had major crushes on Uncle Buck, played by Cameron Mitchell, and wrote him fan mail. I also started, just for fun, to write a storyline for an episode, without, of course, any technical knowledge at all of how to write one. I worked on it in all my spare moments and some which were supposed to be consecrated to other things, like school work.

My burgeoning screenplay was confiscated twice because I was writing it during lessons, once in geography and once in general science. Fortunately I got it back safely on both occasions. When it was finished, Meg asked me what I intended to do with it. I hadn't intended to do anything with it, I'd just written it for our amusement and because I loved the series and writing, in equal measure.

Showing early entrepreneurial flair, Meg said she would market it for me and demanded a ten per cent agent's fee. Because I never thought for a moment she was serious, or that she would succeed, I magnanimously said if she sold it, she could have twenty five per cent. She immediately made me put the offer in writing.

I was helping out at the riding school as usual one Saturday when Meg appeared. She did come from time to time but hadn't been for a long time. She was waving a blue air mail envelope. You could have knocked me down with the proverbial feather to find inside a letter from the executive producer of The High Chaparral, saying complimentary things about my little story and offering a buy-out contract of all rights for the astounding sum of two hundred dollars.

That equated, in those days, to about eighty nine pounds and some shillings. I was at the time earning two shillings and sixpence for working fourteen hour days in the riding school. When I got my first job as a junior reporter some three years or so later, just after decimalisation, my starting wage was thirteen pounds thirty pence a week. Comparatively speaking, it probably still remains the most money for a single short piece of writing I've ever earned.

My school was underwhelmed by such things. They can't have been unaware since, me being the daughter of a local newspaper editor, the story was in all the local papers. But they still called my English "average" on an all-important report when I was in sixth form.

I didn't really have a specific career in mind for much of my time at school, after abandoning the vet idea. I had a sense of fighting the inevitable, aware I would almost certainly finish up in journalism but not wanting to, as it seemed too obvious.

In sixth form we had a series of careers lectures, where people from various professions came and showed us films and gave us talks. I watched one on being an army cadet and thought it looked marvellous. Here were these young women, seemingly doing no work of any description, travelling round the world, having a lot of fun and getting rather well paid for it. Where do I sign?

I was invited to go to the Women's Royal Army Corps, as it was then, Officers' College at Camberley, in Surrey. I travelled down by train and was most impressed to be met at the station by a smart staff car, with a driver who called me ma'am and opened the door for me.

It turned out that the others attending the same weekend and travelling on an earlier train had been collected, as was usual, in a draughty, beaten-up old Land-Rover. But as I was on a later train, I was being picked up by the staff car which was also going to collect various officers who were to attend a dinner night at the college where we were to be staying.

This was my very first encounter with the military at close quarters. Luckily my mother had insisted I travel down in a decent suit, with a skirt, instead of my habitual jeans and a sweat shirt, so I was quite presentable enough to be invited into the house, the home of a major, where I was to wait until other guests had arrived to be collected.

Army officers resplendent in formal mess kit are a rather strange sight, especially as many, depending on their regiments, wear spurs for dress occasions. I was ushered in, given a sherry and a seat, and sat waiting and watching.

The host major, who was quite tall, cut an imposing figure in his tight trousers, shiny patent leather boots, jingling rowelled spurs, ridiculously short, tight fitting, bum-freezing jacket, starched white shirt and bow tie.

He struck a pose by the fireplace, very theatrically consulted his watch and announced: "In thirty seconds, they will be late."

Whilst his wife and the rest of the assembly brayed their condolences, I nearly did the nose trick with my sherry and wondered whether I really could tolerate a life timed to the second.

If the first evening had not been enough to put me off all idea of life as an army cadet, the rest of the weekend certainly did. There seemed to be so many silly rules and traditions that would have been more at home in a girls' boarding school. I'd never been to one but had read everything by Enid Blyton, so felt I had wandered into a chapter of 'In the Fifth at Mallory Towers'.

Amazingly, I was selected as potential officer material (shome mishtake, shurely? Ed.) and invited for a medical. I declined. Politely. So it looked as if it was to be journalism, after all.

I applied for, and was invited to attend an interview for, a twelve-month pre-entry training course in practical journalism, at the Harris Institute, Preston, covering such things as essential law for journalists, which I loved, and public administration, most of which I slept through. Because I was accepted onto the course, though it was no thanks to my school.

My father was well-known in north-west journalism circles, even before he took office as President of the Guild of British Newspaper Editors. Our surname is quite unusual (and it isn't Limejuice!) but I was most anxious that if I got onto the course it was to be on my own merits and not through his name. And in this, the school actually unwittingly helped me.

They were asked to prepared a report on applicants, to be forwarded directly to the National Council for the Training of Journalists, for the use of the interviewing panel. Through some glorious administrative cock-up at my school, my report was sent to me.

It was about as damning as it could possibly be. I quite agreed with their assessment of me as "not suitable for further academic education", but this was, after all, an extremely practical course, to be followed by a three-and-a-half year apprenticeship on a newspaper before qualifying.

But I was furious at the label of "average" for English. I may not have excelled on my A- level English course, although I did achieve a B, but I wasn't hugely inspired by our reading list. And I still maintain it's hardly average to sell a screenplay internationally at age sixteen.

I needed a report from my school in order to go for interview. I was not about to go cap in hand to my school, begging for a better one. So I simply put it into a fresh envelope and sent it off. And attended the interview.

There was a fairly simple, to me, general knowledge paper about the newspaper industry. Unlike some of those present, I knew that a newspaper leader was the editorial, not the editor who wrote it, and other things like that. So I sailed through that section to the formal interview.

It appeared to go not too badly. Then one of the panel said there were impressed with my application but concerned that my school had supplied a not very favourable report.

"I know," I replied, "It's absolutely dire, I've read it. It's not necessarily all true."

Gobsmacked, I think, sums up the panel's collective reaction. I explained what had happened, how I'd come to read the report and why I'd decided to take the risk of sending it on.

To this day I'm convinced that bolshie attitude is what got me the place on the course that led to my qualifying in journalism and working on local papers for nearly ten years after leaving college.

# Part Two: Why

All very interesting, you may well be saying, if you've got this far. Or possibly not. But how do we get from a gaga old lady, a chainsaw wielding drunk, a pretentious dog and a barmy middle-aged writer living in the UK to the promised saga of new life in la belle France? But do remember, I promised only to give you the background leading up to that momentous move.

So let me tell you about the why.

Why we suddenly decided to up sticks and move, en masse, a thousand miles from "home". For which I need to rewind a bit to 2003. And I'll say at the outset, the object of this book is not UK-bashing, in particular not rubbishing everything about the UK health and care services and chanting an Orwell-esque mantra of UK bad, France good.

But it's fact, so has to be said, that one of the primary reasons for our collective decision was our disillusionment with the care Mother received as she got older and more befuddled. And our feelings of powerlessness as she seemed to be sucked into a system that wasn't doing all it could for her, whilst we ourselves were not in a position to do any better.

As with alcoholism, it's not really easy to pinpoint the exact moment when one suspects an elderly person is no longer playing with a full deck of cards. We all tend to get absent-minded as we get older and start to remember more vividly things from the distant past rather than the immediate past. Hands up, honestly, if you've never gone into a room and forgotten completely what you went in there for?

I used to love listening to the antics of Terry Wogan's TOGGS (old geysers and gals) on Radio Two, and even contributed a few myself. My personal favourite was the hot day when I stopped for an ice cream on the way home from work, got back to the car, threw the Magnum ice cream on the passenger seat and bit into my mobile phone.

I noticed Mother was getting a bit muddled, so started to ask her a few questions for context, as I'd seen done on programmes like Casualty and Holby City, essential references for all things medical!

I casually asked her: "Who's the Prime Minister?" (bear in mind this was 2003.)

Mother was having one of her sharp days. She gave me a withering look and replied: "Cherie Blair." Touché, Mother.

She was doing very well up to the moment when she had a fall in the road near to her house. She was toddling back from the shops and tripped over an uneven paving stone, landing literally flat on her face.

Offerton, like so many other parts of Stockport, was not the gently refined area it had once aspired to be. Hoodies and gangs haunted the corners of the roads even there. Luckily for Mother, her fall was seen by some of the no doubt many young boys who are still kind and human enough to help an old lady on the ground rather than rob her of her purse and shopping.

They helped her up, took her to her house, helped her get cleaned up, made her some tea and stayed with her until she had recovered from the shock and assured them she could manage and would be fine.

But the fall really knocked her nerve for going out by herself. And if she couldn't go out, she couldn't shop nor visit her good friend Ruby, who lived nearby. Ruby would visit her and get her bits of shopping. But she was no longer young and her husband had a lot of health problems, so they were not able to do a great deal.

Mother had long since stopped going to the parish church where the AP had been sacristan and a lay reader. It had always been very high church, smells and bells. But in an effort to revive flagging congregations, a younger vicar was drafted in, and instead of singing: "Alban, high in glory shining", the remaining elderly and conservative congregation members of St Alban's were reduced to singing: "Who made rats and bats and cats?"

I always threatened Mother that I would have that played at her funeral.

It was all a bit happy-clappy for Mother, who stopped going. A kind member of the congregation, who had known our family for a long time, continued to visit her and help with shopping but then he, sadly, died. So there was no-one in the local area to help Mother out when she needed it.

Her next-door neighbours, who had been there as long as she had, had long since retired and moved to Northumberland to be closer to their family. The young couple who had taken their place were kind enough in their own way, but they had their own busy lives and simply did not have time to spare to take on a needy, elderly neighbour.

It was becoming clear that she was no longer managing by herself, in particular not managing to eat, even with Meals on Wheels bringing food to her. Nor was she managing to take the vast pile of medication she had been prescribed. So we arranged for home carers to go in four times a day to make sure she ate well, took her pills, kept herself clean and was generally kept an eye on.

Almost all of the carers were very kind and caring people who did the job to the best of their ability and training. But it must be said that the overall standard in terms of initiative and intelligence was alarmingly low. And that extended up to management as well as the troops on the ground.

Mother was still living in the house in Offerton where she had lived since 1954. My brother lived in Kidwelly, South Wales, a good four hours drive away, and I lived near Market Rasen, Lincolnshire, almost two and a half hours away, because of the rural roads. So we weren't exactly on the spot to keep a check ourselves.

I tried to go over every weekend, my brother visited when he could, but it soon became clear that there were serious areas of concern in the care provided. My brother, a very good cook, used to make and plate up meals, label them and leave them in the fridge for the carers to reheat and give to Mother.

But we would often find the meals untouched days later. Worse, there would often be piles of untouched medication left around the house. Some of the medication was for a heart condition, without which Mother was experiencing episodes of dizziness and breathlessness.

There was a book left beside the medication in which the carers were supposed to note everything that occurred on their shift for the benefit of the next carer coming in. My brother and I would always read through the book to keep ourselves in the picture.

One incident which sticks in my mind was almost tragic in its ineptitude, and could so easily have been so, literally. One of the kindest carers, let's call her Mary, was also barely literate. She was the most frequent visitor and tended to do all four visits in a day, several days a week.

One weekend I read the notes she had laboriously printed out: (sic for all)

9 oclok nel as not ate her brekfast

12 oclok nel as not ate her diner

4 oclok nel as not ate er tea

7 oclok nel as gon to bed

Poor Mary. She was the sole carer, visiting at all those times, every day. To whom was she addressing these notes? There was only her to read them. And what was she doing about the fact that Mother appeared to be eating nothing at all? Sadly, the answer to that was nothing, it appeared. We calculated one week that Mother had not eaten a meal in five days.

So we started to make noises, quietly and politely at first, to the home care manager, who promised to visit herself to see what the problem was and address it.

Remember the cock-eyed optimist bit? I actually thought things might improve. Wrong!

We were a bit alarmed to be told that the carers were not actually allowed to help Mother to eat nor to give her her medication. Probably the UK's 'Elf and Safety policy at work once more. They could only put food and medication in front of her for her to take herself.

I tried explaining, politely, that if she could make the connection between seeing pills (hers were always carefully sorted into those day per dose compartments) and taking them, she probably wouldn't be in need of home carers. But to no avail.

I tried pointing out that it was essential that she eat, not only for the obvious reason of preventing an already frail and slight elderly lady losing any more weight – Mother had always been of the, as they say oop north, more meat on a budgie's lips stature. Several of her pills had to be taken after food and could be dangerous if taken on an empty stomach.

Things appeared to settle down for a bit. Then I got a call from the care manager herself, who had taken over some of the home visits. Bear in mind, in considering this exchange, that I was at least two and a half hours away by car, despite the motorway link, because of the time it took me to get to the motorway.

Manager: "I'm sorry to bother you but I'm a bit worried about your mum."

Me: "Oh dear, what seems to be the problem?"

Manager: "Well she's a bit floppy and hard to rouse. I've been trying to get her up but she doesn't seem to respond. And her eyes are rolling back in her head a bit."

Me: (through gritted teeth at this stage) "And how long has this been going on?"

Manager: "Well, I've been here about an hour now and she's not come to very much."

Now I'm someone who is inclined to get sarcastic – very – when under stress or dealing with what I perceive to be idiots. To have such a phone conversation with the manager of carers supposed to be ensuring the health and welfare of my vulnerable elderly mother was bringing out the worst in me. And I'm someone who has been accused of using words as a weapon.

Me: "Well, here's a wild suggestion. Have you thought about calling an ambulance? Because what you describe could quite possibly be a TIA (transient ischemic attack) or even a full-blown stroke."

Because I don't just watch Casualty and Holby. I've also done several very detailed first aid courses and been a First Aid at Work appointed person in several workplaces.

By the time the ambulance had collected Mother and taken her to hospital, I had broken just about every speed limit between Market Rasen and Stockport to catch up with her.

Luckily on this occasion, it was a likely combination of not enough to eat or drink, missing some medication and getting the inevitable UTI (urinary tract infection), the curse of the elderly.

So it wasn't too long before she was able to return home. We jumped up and down on the care manager, spat out the pieces and elicited promises of better things.

Hang on, you're saying, why didn't you either move her in with one of you, or one of you move nearer to her?

Fair question. Not possible.

I'd long proposed moving Mother in to live with me but my brother was opposed to the idea as my house was a bit remote.

Although Mother told me she'd like to come and live with me and would frequently phone and ask to come and visit, it later turned out she was telling her doctor and social worker she didn't like coming to stay with me as it was too isolated and she felt lonely.

This was despite me only being out to work three days a week and paying care-trained friends to come in, spend time with her and ensure she ate on days when I was out. With her state of confusion – although she had not yet been diagnosed as having dementia – Mother could often say one thing to one person and something completely different to another.

My brother's house was completely out of the question. A looming, three-storey former bonded warehouse, with parts of the building dating back a thousand years, if its seven staircases and bewildering layout were not enough to make it very mother unfriendly, the fact that it permanently resembled a building site certainly did.

And as for moving nearer - well, by this time house prices in all parts of Cheshire had gone off the Richter scale. So there was no way I could realise enough equity on my humble Lincolnshire abode to get a toe-hold in Cheshire. And valuing my independence and country living so much, I really didn't relish the prospect of moving back to live with Mother.

So for the time being we decided it was best to soldier on as best we could, checking up as frequently as we could between us.

We were very alarmed on one occasion when a carer pushed a note through the door to say they'd called, got no reply so gone away, without taking any action to find out why there was no reply.

Then the inevitable happened. Another call from the care manager to say she'd arrived to find Mother had fallen, had apparently spent the night on the floor and was complaining of back pain.

She said she'd got her upstairs and put her to bed but she was still complaining of back pain.

I tried very hard not to go off the deep end to hear that a care manager had moved an elderly patient with osteoporosis, complaining of back pain, following a fall, and again instructed her to call an ambulance while I once more broke a few speed limits crossing the Pennines.

Luckily, no bones broken, but it was becoming clear that Mother was getting increasingly confused. And there was another consideration. I was due to go on a sponsored trail ride in the Canadian Rockies to raise money for Guide Dogs for the Blind, at the same time as my brother was going to be out of the country. This meant neither of us would be around to keep a close eye on Mother's care. Was it time to consider the unthinkable and put her into a home?

Her social worker, who was absolutely brilliant and very helpful, arranged a pre-discharge meeting at the hospital to discuss what was best for her, which I was to attend as my brother was not available. I was very disconcerted when I arrived at the appointed time to find no medical staff from the hospital were available to discuss Mother's health or requirements.

Worse, Mother was lying in bed with bright vivid red cheeks, rather wild-eyed, and for the first time ever, not able to recognise me. When her social worker asked her who I was, she said: "I don't know, I've never seen that lady before."

I drew this to the attention of the staff nurse on duty who assured me that Mother was fine. I pointed out she didn't appear to know who I was or where she was. The nurse again assured me she was fine and said to Mother: "Do you know who I am?"

Mother replied: "You're a nurse."

"You see, she's fine," the nurse assured me.

"You don't just think the nurse's uniform might be a bit of a give-away?" I asked.

"But she knows where she is," came the response. "Do you know where you are, Nell?"

To which Mother responded: "In hospital."

Another triumphant reply. "There you are, she knows where she is."

With teeth gritted to the point of lockjaw I asked: "Have you asked her which hospital she's in?"

When asked, Mother happily replied "St Helens", with great triumph, as if she'd just scored maximum points on Mastermind.

Now St Helens was Mother's home town and she had certainly not been in its hospital for probably fifty years or more.

It got worse. A doctor was summoned, who concurred with the nurse that Mother was fine, her mind was fine, all was well. The doctor was an Asian, with quite a pronounced accent. And that is not a racist remark, it is just an observation on the fact that his accent was hard for me to follow and I am not deaf nor was I confused due to clearly running a high fever.

He asked her: "What is name of queen?" (sic)

I was tempted to mutter "Freddie Mercury, Brian May ..." but Mother, again as triumphantly as a child mastering her two times table said "Queen Elizabeth."

It's worth remembering that the current monarch became queen in 1952, a time when Mother was in possession of all of her marbles. I had somehow expected a doctor in charge of whatever it's now politically correct to call a geriatric ward to see the relevance of the fact that she knew the name of the monarch but not of her own daughter.

Finally, a few days later, when both my brother and I visited the hospital and voiced our concerns, we were finally given a long list of what was wrong with Mother, including vascular dementia. Not Alzheimer's disease, mercifully, but definitely a lot of impairment of the mental faculties.

It's incredible how many people, even health care professionals, automatically think dementia equals Alzheimers. It doesn't. But vascular dementia brings problems of its own. Short term memory simply packs up its suitcase, leaves on the midnight train and never even pops back for a visit.

Recent events in Mother's life had been wiped from the memory banks and could not be restored. Whereas things from her distant past remained as vivid as the day they were learned, so were trotted out more and more frequently, rather like a security blanket.

As Mother herself said frequently: "Mother, Mother, it's a bugger. Sell the pig and buy me OUT," which got more and more emphatic each time she said it.

We were also told she had myeloma, cancer of the plasma cells, but were reassured that given her age and the normally slow progression of the disease, she was likely to die with it rather than from it. If that news can be called reassuring.

So with the help of her lovely social worker, we set about finding her at least a temporary place in a home to cover my brother's and my absence from the country.

We put her into the home. It was all right but nothing special. It was in quite a rough area of Stockport. On my first visit, I was a bit alarmed when two quite young boys, barely into their teens, stopped me and asked me where they could buy drugs, and didn't appear to be joking.

Whenever either my brother or I visited, we always took Mother out in the car on one of the picnics she enjoyed or to experience the other things she loved, like mooching round the charity shops. She was reasonably happy there but, and this is where you can all jump all over me and accuse me of being a snob, it wasn't really her social level. It was a bit beer and skittles and Mother was more wine and croquet.

So we decided to move her to St Helens, her home town, to the very nice home where her older sister Ethel (fashion buyer turned home maker, made her own knickers) was now living. It was a completely different home altogether, rather like a refined small hotel, beautifully decorated and furnished, with lots of little side rooms where residents could entertain visiting family and friends.

There, as soon as a relative or visitor arrived, a member of staff would bring them a tray of tea and biscuits, with real china, cups and sauces, not clumpy mugs. All the residents were well groomed, smartly dressed, none of the wet drawers and all-pervading smell of pee of the other home. Mother settled in very well with her older sister to talk to, and adjoining bedrooms, like in their youth. Sighs of relief all round.

Then Auntie Ethel died. She suffered a major stroke, battled on in hospital for two weeks as she was always a fighter, then gave up the ghost. She was ninety-three.

Dementia brings its own blessings. After asking on the first day where Ethel was, Mother appeared to forget all about the fact that they had been there together and seen each other every day. I did tell her what had happened and she had a little weep, but then forgot all about it.

I also took her to the funeral service at Christ Church, Eccleston, where the family had worshipped for years and where Auntie Ethel was to be buried with her mother, father and unmarried brother Harold. We got there early as Mother by now needed a wheelchair to get around in and it took a bit of manoeuvring to get it out of the car, her into it and negotiate the way into the church.

The church looked beautiful, with lovely white flowers everywhere. Auntie would have approved. As we waited for the service to begin, Mother looked round then asked me: "Is Ethel going to be here?"

How to answer that?

* * *

Despite losing her sister, Mother continued to do well at the home for a while. But she then started to have episodes of dehydration and other associated conditions, and had a couple of falls which necessitated hospital stays. That's when we discovered that things in the UK hospital system left a lot to be desired.

After one fall, the home phoned to inform me that she had been taken to hospital with pain in her right hip. I phoned the hospital, who were incredibly unhelpful and said they couldn't discuss Mother's case with me over the phone because of that good old chestnut "patient confidentiality". But they did say surgery might be necessary.

I pointed out to them that because of Mother's dementia, my brother and I now held joint power of attorney for her and if they even thought about putting her under the knife without our consent, there would be repercussions.

So instead of the weekly trips to the home, I was going instead to the hospital. And getting very exasperated to find medication not given, meals left untouched out of her reach and, most memorable of all, the day when she was taken to hospital with a suspected fractured head of the right femur. When I arrived, I found Mother had been placed sitting upright in her bedside chair, clearly in a lot of pain.

It transpired that the decision to sit her up in the chair was based on a clear X-ray of the left hip – not the one she had fallen on and not the one that was causing her the pain.

I also had to experience one of the annoying and all too frequent happenings at UK hospitals now, exorbitant car park charges for visitors and nowhere else within sensible walking distance to leave a car.

And as the hospital trips, falls and other problems started to increase, the nice home, which was a care home, not a nursing home, began to make noises about no longer being able to meet all of Mother's needs.

It was time to take drastic measures.

# Part Three: Where

I'm not sure when I started thinking longingly of a future life in France, but it certainly pre-dated our problems with Mother by a few years.

As the new millennium had rolled into view, a close friend and I were talking about maybe getting a place together there, and I started buying various French property magazines and skimming through to see what was out there. We event went to a French property exhibition together up in Harrogate, towing a rickety old caravan lent by a friend, in which to spend the night.

My French wasn't too terrible, I could get by adequately in most situations, although my grammar was, and still is, pretty atrocious.

We had a very nice French teacher in middle school, who was far too soft to be put in charge of a mob of school-girls, especially with an unfortunate name like Mrs Twitchett.

Whenever she began a lesson by proposing we should do anything remotely grammatical, we always begged and pleaded to be taught French songs instead. Which is why, to this day, I know all of the words to traditional songs like "Chevaliers de la table ronde" and "Il pleut, il pleut, bergère " but can only make a wild stab at the subjunctive of anything other than the verb to go.

As a teenager I'd made two school exchange trips, to Tournon sur Rhône in the Ardèche department of the Rhône-Alpes region, and loved it. The first time, aged sixteen, my best friend Meg and I were billeted with families in the same road. But goodness knows what had been going through the head of the teacher who matched us up with our pen friends and their respective accommodation.

I stayed in a very smart apartment above the droguerie, where my pen friend and I were very well looked after by a maid, while her parents worked downstairs in the shop. The maid did all my washing and ironing for me, kept my room, which I had to myself, tidy and spotless, and presented us with delicious meals.

Poor Meg stayed with the greengrocer's family across the road, where she shared a room with her pen-friend, which the male members of the family had to walk through to get to other parts of the house.

The sanitary facilities were of the decidedly archaic type which were once so typical of French camp sites – the kind of booby-trapped open floor-level toilet which I believe is called a Turkish crapper, without intending any offence to anyone Turkish in case I've got that wrong! With very rudimentary washing facilities down in the cellar of the property.

They were a delightful and extremely hospitable family, who did everything within their power to make Meg feel welcome. One day, in my digs, I was presented with a meal which, I was assured, Meg had pronounced delicious, her favourite. To me, it resembled nothing more than a dubious object made from what appeared to be an old string vest gone blue with mould.

Curse the British politesse which had made Meg say she loved it when, in fact, she hated it, and me to do likewise, resulting it being served almost every day, as a special treat.

On my second stay, I was hosted by a very large, very loud liberal college lecturer who didn't even realise that his daughter was spending every spare moment bonking the son of the local wine merchant.

Because neither family was aware of the liaison, they didn't know they needed to coordinate their trips away more carefully. One wonderful, memorable weekend, both sets of parents managed to absent themselves at the same time for a long weekend.

The party started at a bar in town, where we bought copious quantities of cheap red wine, then walked through the streets to the boyfriend, Bruno's, flat, drinking as we went. The group my pen-friend hung around with were known collectively as "la bande", the gang. or sometimes as "les hippies", as they favoured long hair and facial hair – mostly the boys, but not exclusively – and wore hairy Afghan coats, and very old jeans, and smelled of wood smoke and patchouli oil.

Someone alleged to know which apartment Bruno lived in – clearly my pen-friend had never been there because of the taboo nature of the liaison. France in the late sixties was still very constrained, though not as much as it had been, and there were rules, even for the daughter of a liberal lecturer.

So "la bande" swarmed up the stairs of the large old building which was sub-divided into spacious flats, knocked briefly on a door and swept in without waiting for an invite, since doors in that part of France in those days were hardly ever locked. By this time there was already not much left of the wine, so we were all a bit merry.

It very quickly became clear that the two rather bewildered elderly ladies eyeing us with great suspicion were not actually anything to do with Bruno and we'd gone up too many steps to the apartment above.

I'm not sure how long we stayed at Bruno's place. I don't remember much of that part of the weekend. Not much at all, in fact, after someone found the key to Bruno's father's wine cellar and we found the very expensive mature export whiskey in there.

But at some point we must all have decamped back to Martine's house and I must have gone on the back of someone's motorbike because I do have a hazy memory of leaning back slightly whilst being driven at terrifying speeds and trying to work out the significance of the word Yahama or Yahamma or Yamhamma or something, on the back of the leather jacket in front of me. It seemed to change every time I tried to read it through bleary eyes.

The party continued at Martine's parents' empty house. At one point, even I had had enough of the drinking and carousing, so I vaguely remember going out for a walk and wandering into a nearby church to stagger in semi-inebriated admiration round the stations of the cross.

I have another vague memory of sloping off to my bedroom for a sleep after a refreshing shower and hair wash, only to wake up to find an unidentified male sleeping in my penfriend's bed in the same room. No-one was ever able accurately to say who that might have been. Just another gatecrasher, no doubt.

Martine, all this time, was busy in her parents' bed with Bruno. In fact the party was going on so long and so well that we all only just woke up a very short time before the parents arrived back, and were still racing round frantically cleaning up and tidying away when they returned.

We had several days of their absence to account for. I was given the task of telling them how we'd passed the time. I'm not sure that my lame tale of doing the stations of the cross and washing our hair quite did the trick.

So I'd always had a hankering to go back to France, preferably to rural France, as one of the great things about "la bande" was that after school, we would all pile into a collection of identical old Citroen 2CVs, clutching bags of pain au chocolat, and drive up into the hills to an old ruined farmhouse which had become their hang-out.

The identical 2CVs nearly cost me my flight back to the UK, at yet another drunken party, this time on the banks of the river Rhône. I'd stuffed my shoulder bag, containing my passport and all my travel documents, for safe keeping, into what I thought was the car I'd arrived in and so would be going home in.

Only it turned out to belong to someone only on the fringes of "la bande" who was due to leave the following morning to start his national service. It was only by trawling all the cafés and bars in town that we found him just in time before he departed with my bag, containing my train and plane tickets and everything else vital for my return trip, still in the back of his car.

I had a vague dream of going back to where I'd had such fun in my teenage years. But by keeping a weather eye on the regional prices in the magazines and by then on the new, to me, and wonderful phenomenon known as t'internet, I knew that area was going to be outside my budget.

And then there was a song buzzing round in the back of my mind. Those of you who may remember an advert for Dubonnet in, I think, the seventies, with the strapline "Dubonnet - way up there," will know the one I mean. It was the hauntingly beautiful shepherd's song Bailero, from Canteloube's Songs of the Auvergne.

To my mind, any region which could produce music as outstanding as that had to be worth visiting. So in 2004, I asked my best friend Jill, with whom I usually holidayed, if she fancied a change from our usual trail riding trips to go for a drive round the Auvergne.

It turned out she'd already been. Jill's a very intrepid traveller and has been to most places, usually on the back of a horse. Great Wall of China? Oh yes, I've ridden alongside that. Russian steppes? Oh yes, I've ridden across there. The Auvergne's Puy de Dôme volcano? Oh yes, I've ridden up that. But all said in the best possible taste.

Nevertheless, she was quite happy to come with me and do some B&B hopping round three of the Auvergne's départements, the Puy de Dôme, Cantal and Haute Loire. Jill is not only my very best mate, with whom I've been through some pretty exciting adventures, she is also essential to me on any foreign travel because I'm absolutely petrified of flying.

It's something that runs in the family. My brother is as well. Our father, in the wartime, wanted to stay close to home so joined the RAF, as there was a base very near to Prescot, where he lived with his parents. His much more adventurous younger brother wanted to see the world, so he joined the Navy.

In typical ironic fashion, Uncle was posted to Liverpool, a short hop from his home, whilst Father was sent to Africa and discovered on the long flight how much he actually hated flying. He spent his war years in what was then Rhodesia, as a court stenographer for courts martial as, being a journalist, he had good shorthand and typing speeds. And there he stayed until he was invalided out after being stung on the foot by a scorpion. I know. You couldn't make it up.

Jill's father had been a wartime bomber pilot, and later a commercial airline pilot. So Jill has flown all over the world and is always very calm and knows all the tricks of how to avoid being bumped, how to get an upgrade and other useful stuff.

Above all, she has the most reassuring manner imaginable to deal with my frequent panic attacks. She always has something totally convincing to say, and whereas the logical part of my brain knows she's probably telling porkies, it does wonders in helping to keep my heart rate down to a manageable two hundred beats per minute.

I could be climbing the walls screaming "Oh my god, one of the engines has just fallen off!" and Jill would probably just calmly reply: "No, that's perfectly normal on this type of aircraft, they just jettison one of them to alter the trim to prepare for landing." And I'd believe her!

So in April 2004, we set off together for a whistle-stop tour round the Auvergne. As I had loads of spare Air Miles, we opted to fly Heathrow to Lyon, in what turned out to be, to me, a very small plane that didn't quite look up to the job.

It also turned out they didn't have the means to provide me with the vegetarian meal I had ordered. The choice was beef or turkey ham. I complained. I was hungry. It's not as if I could pop out to the nearest takeaway. Air France told me that although they had accepted my booking for a vegetarian meal, that didn't mean they were contracted to supply it.

Luckily such an attitude didn't seem to apply to the aircraft, which appeared to have all its requisite engines and technical things, since it got us there safely, despite looking like an over-grown locust on the tarmac next to proper sized planes.

Jill and I have been good friends since the early 1980s when I had a riding centre in Wales and she came first for hacking, then bought a horse which she kept at livery with me. We get on incredibly well together – believers might say it's because we're both Leos, so kindred spirits.

It's a measure of such a close bond that, having arranged to meet at the appropriate terminal at Heathrow, me driving down from Lincolnshire, she across from West Wales, we managed to park in the next row to one another in the enormous long-stay car park within five minutes of one another, without any plans to do so.

Jill had left choosing and booking the B&Bs up to me as I had more time for research than she did. She teaches agriculture, so as we both like the country and all things animal, I'd opted for mostly farm-style accommodation. Our first night was to be at a dairy goat farm in the Bois Noir (Black Wood) north of Thiers.

It was around Easter and, with glorious memories of hot sunshine in the Rhône valley in those school-days of old, I'd packed my zip-offs and roll-back-sleeve shirts in anticipation of a sun-tan. As we turned off the motorway and began to climb amongst sinister trees, we began to encounter snow. Rather a lot of it.

We battled on regardless, with Jill map-reading from the instructions the B&B proprietor had sent us, but it soon became clear we were now hopelessly lost. We reassured ourselves confidently that there were no longer wolves in these woods. But it was very dark and we were by now both tired and hungry.

Luckily we came across one of those French country bars in the middle of nowhere, the ones where you can't imagine where their clientèle comes from or how they keep going. The exclusively male gathering looked amused as two middle-aged ladies trudged in out of the snow asking for directions. But they were happy to help put us on the right road and even wrote out directions for us on the back of a beer mat.

By now it was extremely dark, the roads were covered with snow and I was having to drive very slowly in our little hired Corsa. And we were discovering a fact of rural French living. Neither roads nor houses have names on them. Only the hamlets themselves are named, so when you reach a cluster of houses you have to get out and check the family name on each letter box to find your destination.

On one such descent, Jill found a tiny sign pointing to our B&B. So while she trotted ahead on foot, I attempted to make a multi-point turn in the little car and managed to ground it on a frozen rut. There were some disgusting crunching noises in extricating it, but before long we were ushered into a lovely warm farmhouse kitchen, with a log fire roaring in the big open grate and a feast spread on the long wooden table.

Even more incredibly for France, and especially for the meat-loving Auvergne, they'd catered to my almost-vegetarian diet, with a lovely cheesy pastry, hard boiled eggs in a cheese sauce, a big bowl of tabouleh and lots of goats' cheese, of course, with various bits of dead animal on offer for carnivore Jill, and a delicious sachertorte for both of us to follow.

Our host was absolutely hilarious and regaled us and the other guests, a Belgian couple, teachers, who both spoke good English but we all preferred to speak French, for hours with his funny stories. Our first experience of the Auvergne was a very positive one.

We'd decided to see as much of the region as possible in a short time, so opted to stay only one night in each B&B. It was with some regret we left the comfort and hospitality of our first hostelry the following morning and set off for the region's capital, Clermont-Ferrand.

It has to be said, with its almost black volcanic rock cathedral and sprawling agglomeration, Clermont is not a very prepossessing city viewed from afar.

I find cities resistable at the best of times and although Jill is a Londoner born and bred, she agreed that we should give it a swerve and head off further afield to see the area's other attractions, the volcanoes, including the largest of which, the Puy-de-Dôme, at 1,465 metres, which lends its name to the département.

It was then that we discovered how very short the Auvergne tourist season is. The coach which took passengers on a white-knuckle ride to the summit didn't run until much later in the year, and the road, which was occasionally open to traffic, was currently closed for logging operations. So we contented ourselves with a pleasant walk, despite little flurries of snow and sleet, through the beech woods at its base, then headed off to explore the next corner of the region.

We stopped to look at a château on our way. Guess what? Yes, you've cottoned on already. Only open during the summer. So we arrived at our next accommodation in daylight, probably much to the relief of the poor hire car.

*The Puy de Dome, one of the Auvergne's iconic landmarks, wearing a dusting of snow.*

Our bedroom had a spectacular view straight onto the snow-covered Puy-de-Dôme and despite not having the heating on, it was so well insulated it was absolutely boiling.

This time our fellow visitors were three French families, one with children, who in typical French fashion ate at the table with us and seemed to stay awake an incredibly long time, well after we were both flagging and nodding over our chocolate mousse with hazelnut meringue.

One couple decided to treat us to tales of some of their holiday adventures. Just my luck, as they decided to tell us the story of what happened to them when they went on what I think they said was the world's highest cable car, somewhere in

South America. And it broke down. At its highest point. Over a canyon.

And one of the reasons I hate flying so much is that I'm acrophobic - I'm afraid of heights. Height is a relative term. For some people it may be a cable car. For others, like me, it's more than six rungs up a ladder. So listening to their long and dramatic tale was a form of torture to me. Especially when they got to the part where the only way to recover the passengers from the crippled car was for special forces to abseil down from a helicopter and transfer them in some sort of wicker basket. <Hands over ears, la-la-la> One occasion when I wished my French hadn't been up to following a conversation.

When planning our trip, I'd described roughly a circular shape round the Auvergne, going anti-clockwise. Those of you interested in witchcraft may well think it significant that voluntarily turning anti-clockwise, or widdershins, was an old way of identifying a witch.

So we drove on further south into the next département, the Cantal, which seemed even less populated than the Puy-de-Dôme and had a lot of the designated "Most Beautiful Villages of France".

We even found a spectacular château on a lake and were amazed to find it open, so took the guided door. I was probably so shocked that it was open I even managed to go up the tower, although I didn't dare peep out of any arrow slits on the way up or down.

Our hostess that evening introduced us to a local speciality, a liqueur made from the flowers of the gentians which grow everywhere around the area. Not the pretty blue alpines you find in gardens but gentiana lutea, the great yellow gentian or mountain gentian. It produces a liquid that looks a little like your granny's favourite cough remedy. Although that probably tasted nicer. It is, as the French say, un peu spéciale, not to everyone's taste. I would imagine it makes a very effective killer of woodworm or a timber preservative.

And for the benefit of anyone visiting France and unfamiliar with the language, that is not a good parallel to draw, since préservatif is the French word for a condom.

The best way of seeing any area is usually to get up as high as you can, and as high as acrophobia will allow you to, and drink in the views. So the next day we headed for the Puy Mary, part of an ancient volcano which is Europe's largest strato-volcano. But it was a bit of a "snow stopped play" sort of day, as heavy snow prevented us from following our chosen route over the top and down the other side.

We opted instead for a short walk in crisp, white, knee-deep drifts and were thrilled at the distant sighting of what my wildlife book told us could very well have been a genet, the little spotted wild cats which inhabit the area.

Another château, which was amazingly also open, and this time I was goaded into going up the tower since two of the other visitors, Catalans, were both well into their eighties but still managed to get within one flight of stairs of the top. So I had to go one better, of course, and climbed the final flight with wobbly, knocking knees.

All of this walking in the snow was very dehydrating, and although we'd both gone armed with plenty of SPF cream, I hadn't thought to take any lip salve, expecting to be fighting off sunburn rather than windburn. So at the next town we made a trip to the pharmacie where I did one of my legendary mix-ups of two very similar sounding French words.

Lèvre is the French for lip, not lièvre, which is a hare. No wonder the pharmacist looked at me a little oddly. It can't be every day his shop is invaded by strange middle-aged foreign tourists attempting to buy balm to put on the poor bunny-wunnies in the mountains.

We made our leisurely way across the southern edge of the Cantal and on into the third département of our travels, the Haute-Loire, for a look at the pretty town of Le-Puy-en-Velay, where every sticking up point of volcanic rock seems to have at least a statue of the blessed virgin, if not a church, erected on its summit. It's a UNESCO World Heritage Site and also a departure point for the pilgrim route to Santiago de Compostela.

And for those of you who have heard that Paris is the dog poo capital of France, I can tell you with some authority – it's not. Never in my life have a seen such a collection of dog poo. There was scarcely a centimetre of pavement to walk on which didn't have a pile of dog-do's on it. And this despite a number of designated dog loos, which were overflowing with the stuff.

We indulged our horsey side in this area, visiting a very interesting equine museum with the woolliest, curliest donkey I've ever seen, and spending the evening as paying guests of a young German woman who ran a riding centre nearby. She and I swapped riding centre horror stories in a mixture of French and German till late into the evening.

Then it was time to be heading back towards Lyon for our return flight. And I'd routed our return to take us through Tournon, where I'd been on the school exchanges, and St Vallier-sur-Rhône, where Meg and I had passed that first memorable holiday in France.

Going back is always a risk. What I'd remembered as a small, sleepy town was now bustling and traffic-jammed. The surrounding hills where I'd been with "la bande" were now sprinkled with boring new-builds.

The decision was made for me. Once the time came to head for France, it would almost certainly be to the wide open green spaces of the Auvergne.

* * *

But I'm a belt and braces sort of person. I like to have at least a Plan B for everything in life, including the mundane. And I'm happiest if I have up to a Plan Q in reserve, just in case.

The Auvergne had really won my heart. But I often find the best way to find out how much you like something is to expose yourself to something completely different, to compare and contrast.

One part of my chequered career involved working with young people with learning disabilities, through the medium of horses. Fascinating stuff. I was a vocational coordinator, a posh job title (which I was allowed to make up for myself) for finding them work experience placements, sending them out there and doing visits to check up that all was going well.

These were highly horse motivated young people. In most cases motivated by absolutely nothing else. So my idea was for each to do two work experience sessions, one in a horse-related environment, the other doing something completely different.

They were packed off to work in local supermarkets, to help out in cafés and at nurseries. One, with an almost photographic memory for train timetables, spent a blissful few days helping British Rail. They were allowed to suggest their own fantasy workplace and it if was remotely within my power, I organised it for them.

Finding a work experience placement with a dentist proved to be about my biggest "Jim'll Fix It" type challenge. But I met lovely Robin through the French evening class we both attended and he was delighted to help. So young David had a wonderful few days, as he told us enthusiastically: "watching people having their teeth distracted."

So applying my own theory, I thought I'd better go and have a look at another part of France, just to see if it confirmed my passion for the Auvergne.

I instantly dismissed Dordogneshire because of its high British ex-pat population. Not that I'm anti Brit. I'm seventy-five per cent one myself. I just don't see the point in leaving one country and going to live in another surrounded by residents of the one you've just left.

Trawling the Internet looking at house prices threw up the Limousin as a possible. My means were very modest so it needed to be something cheap. I still had the money I'd inherited from Auntie, salted away in an online account, but it wasn't much, just enough for a deposit. And I'm not quite enough of a cock-eyed optimist to sell my little house in Market Rasen before being sure I would settle happily in France.

A word about my little Lincolnshire cottage. When I moved up to the area from Dorset, having never been there before, I rented a very pleasant former council house in a small, very much sought-after village nestling on one of the prettiest parts of the Lincolnshire Wolds.

For those who don't know the county, which seems to be about ninety per cent of the population of England, despite its size, Lincolnshire is not exclusively flat, although large tracts of it are. The Wolds are delightful rolling chalk uplands, and the area around my little cottage was a designated Area of Outstanding Natural Beauty – and rightly so.

I wasn't particularly thinking of buying a property at this stage in my life, and certainly was not certain that the area was where I wanted to put down long-term roots, having been there barely six months. But, like the Elephant's Child, I am full of "'satiable curtiosity".

So when a neighbour told me horror stories of a cottage in the hamlet that was coming up for sale, I simply had to go and take a look at it. She told me it had been repossessed by the mortgage company when the former occupant, who apparently had some mental health issues, fell behind with payments and became unable to live there on her own any more.

According to my source, the house was in very poor condition, as she'd kept all of her animals indoors for years – and I do mean all. Apparently the menagerie included dogs, cats, chickens and goats. It seems that a firm of commercial cleaners had been sent to at least make it presentable enough to be put on the market.

The next door neighbour said a couple of young men swaggered up the path to the back door full of bravado (these particular ex farm workers' cottages only had one door, at the back of the house). June, my neighbour, called a friendly greeting over the fence and warned them of the horrors they were to face.

They were all macho, full of tales of the terrible sights they'd seen and how they were ready for anything. She said they must have lasted inside for all of about five minutes before they left and refused to go back.

A second company came with power washers and simply blasted eleven years of accumulated dirt out as best they could, but that was the extent of the cleaning and preparation for sale which had taken place. Not quite House Doctor!

I had my mother and Auntie Ethel staying with me at the time, this being 1997, before either of them started to lose their marbles, necessitating going into a home. I decided it would be fun to take them to see this house of horrors. I didn't even know which estate agent was marketing it, as there was not yet a board up, but as there were not many agents in Market Rasen, I set off to ask around.

I knew very little about the property, I'd just walked past it with Meic a few times on our voyages of discovery around the area and thought it looked nice, and it was in a pleasant location, down a cart track, opposite a large farm yard.

Luckily I hit gold at the first estate agent's I went into. They had just that very day taken instruction to sell, had the keys somewhere <much rummaging round to find them> but had not yet had chance to prepare any detailed sales particulars.

Armed with the keys, off we set, the two old dears and I, and we duly trundled up to the door of the property and turned the key.

It's hard to say which of our senses was assaulted first. The smell was indescribable. But my eye was immediately drawn to the tell-tale dark brown stains all over the floors and the door frames, wherever we looked.

*Perhaps not surprisingly, the surveyor who did the report
on my grottage for mortgage purposes, described it as
"unfit for human habitation".*

Before we'd even stepped over the threshold, Mother was already saying "No, oh no." But Auntie, who was surprisingly intrepid, was bumbling about peeping into rooms and cupboards and following me up the stairs and round the bedrooms – very brave, as parts of the upstairs floor boards had been rotted away with presumably several years' accumulation of animal urine.

It was surprisingly roomy, with three sensible sized bedrooms and a bathroom, though for those readers of a delicate nature, I won't dwell too much on the stains in the bath. My neighbour only told me their origin later on when the house was mine. I might tell you about it at some point, but I'll give you a Twilight Zone type klaxon warning before doing so.

It was quirky and cottagey, with windows coming down quite low towards the floor, and a random window from the second bedroom overlooking the stairs, which made it very much lighter than it might otherwise have been.

Mother was still "no, no-ing" in the distance somewhere, but intrepid Auntie said: "This is very you. It could be lovely, and so light."

So we drove back into town to hand in the keys and I made an offer on the spot of very slightly under the asking price, which was very reasonable for the area, even considering the amount of work that would need to be done. And my offer was accepted.

After so much time, effort and money invested in one little grottage, as I affectionately called my grotty cottage until it took shape, I wasn't in any hurry to let it go until I really needed to and until I knew I'd found something of which I would become equally as fond.

So, still very much in the planning stage, it was heigh-ho for the open roads of Limousin, on another voyage of discovery. And this time I decided to be incredibly brave and go on my own – on a plane. My first ever solo flight. Jill was probably off to Iceland or India or Africa or somewhere for her half-term break.

I caught a cheap flight from Stansted to Limoges, with apologies to all those who will now be singing the Fascinating Aïda song of the same name for the rest of the day. It wasn't too terrible, but as usual with these budget airlines, the airport was a little out of the way and there was no public transport into town, so it had to be a taxi.

I'd booked into a cheap and cheerful hotel close to the railway station so I could easily embark on the next part of my adventure the following day. So cheap and cheerful that at breakfast time, it transpired, they barely ran to crockery. You simply put your sliced bread, which was all that was on offer, on your tray and ate from that.

I decided to while away the time before my train by visiting the cathedral. Cock-eyed optimism again? Yep. Closed for repairs. It was long past the main tourist season. But I did find a very nice botanical garden with lots of interesting plants, many still in bloom, where I encountered a very amusing black cat who insisted on giving me the guided tour. He would walk in front of me for a while, disappear into the undergrowth, then pop out of the bushes next to some plant he felt particularly worthy of my attention.

At the station I got very brave and rode up the exterior glass-sided lift. Okay, it's only one storey, but those of you who also have acrophobia will know the significance of this courageous act.

From browsing the 'net for interesting places to visit, I'd settled on a small town called Guéret, in the Creuse département, because if there's one wild animal I've always wanted to see up close and personal it's a wolf, although I've heard one howl in the Canadian Rockies. And not far from Guéret is a wolf park called Les Loups de Chabrière.

I'd wanted to make my trip as green as possible. I'd thought of going by ferry, either taking my fairly inoffensive small Golf, or as a foot passenger. But when I looked at prices from Hull, my nearest port, I thought they were quoting me for a share in the shipping company not a return ticket, and the long drive down to Dover was not appealing on either practical or environmental grounds.

So instead I took the cheap flight (Diddly aiden daidin daidin dai) but drove to Stansted airport because: "a taxi to the arse of the world was more than a hundred pound." If you haven't heard the song before, you're going to have to Google it now, aren't you?

And part of my mission to be greener involved renting a bike from the tourist office. Optimism? Moi? It was years and years since I'd ridden a bike. And I'd never done a lot of it nor been particularly good at it.

There was the memorable occasion when I'd been biking from main school to the annexe of Stockport High School for Girls, where I was a reluctant pupil, for a violin lesson (not enthusiastic about that either; you may remember I only took it up as violin lessons clashed with the school sport of lacrosse, which I hated with a passion). Cycling with my violin across the handlebars caused me to lose balance and crash, scraping my bum along the tarmac and taking off a layer of skin.

Our young, male violin teacher decided, very wisely, even in the 1960s, when nobody gave a thought to such things, that administering first aid to a female pupil's posterior was well outside his remit, so he summoned my mate Meg, who nobly stuck a plaster on it for me.

You know someone is truly a good friend when they'll stick a plaster on your bum.

So I turned up at the tourist office to collect my trusty bike, which turned out to have a very uncomfortable saddle, or at least one not designed for my particular anatomy, and I was used to spending longs hours in the saddle of a horse. And, rucksack on my back, off I wobbled to find the B&B I had booked.

It was called Le Cottage and looked like a witch's house from a fairy tale, low eaves drooping over small windows, rather dark, and with lots of trees and shrubs close by, cutting out the natural daylight.

Lots of homes in central France are specifically designed to keep out as much sunlight as possible, which seems strange to Anglo-Saxon minds. But although it's not hot all year round, when it gets hot it can get overpowering, so all that is possible is done to keep the houses cool inside.

My bedroom was a delight; big, blowsy floral print wallpaper over every conceivable surface including the ceiling, creaky old wooden floorboards and a dinky little toilet in a tiny cubbyhole which required some imagination to use without being decapitated, even for my modest stature.

A very kind and helpful landlady gave me vouchers for a reduced meal in town that night, as she didn't provide evening meals, and kindly locked away my bike, berating the tourist office for not giving me an anti-theft device for it and insisting I go back the next day to demand one. She even produced a sort of crocheted doily which she offered to make the seat less uncomfortable. It made not a jot of difference. It didn't even stay in place. But it was a very kind gesture.

There were, she told me, other residents, but they were there to collect mushrooms in the woods so would be up and gone before 3am. Each to their own.

The house was well kept but with an all-pervading smell of cat pee, which made me nostalgic for the early days of my grottage. Breakfast the following morning was copious, all home made, and delicious. Proper bread, unlike the sliced of the Limoges hotel, home made butter, home made cherry jam and a wonderful cake made from hazelnuts. I pocketed a slice of that for my elevenses later on.

Even for my taste, the tea was like weasel water. When I was a young cub reporter, I drank tea you could easily have trotted a mouse across. But my palette changed over the years and I now prefer it much weaker. I thought Madame said it was thé Earl, or Earl Grey tea, but realised afterwards it was tilleul, from lime trees, the broad-leaved lime, not the citrus variety, much drunk by the French for its calming properties.

After such sustenance, it was time to head off to see the wolves, on a lovely warm autumnal day, which made the prospect of a bike ride very pleasant indeed. I had my map, but Madame the landlady insisted on telling me a short-cut. I learned the hard way that this is a strange trait, not just of Creusoises but many other French – to be a bit liberal in their interpretation of short-cuts and directions in general.

I seemed to go quite a long way and was soon into broad-leaf and conifer woodland very similar to Wales' Brechfa Forest region, where I had lived for eight years. Bizarrely, the forest tracks were littered with the bodies of many dead black and yellow salamanders. To this day I have no idea why.

I eventually came to a sign which said " Les Loups de Chabrière – 3kms". Much encouraged, as I was starting to flag, not being cycling fit, I picked up the pace and pedalled and walked for rather a long time (walking because some of the up-hills were beyond my levels of fitness on the bike.) Then I came to another sign – which said exactly the same thing and quoted exactly the same distance. No doubt a French in-joke.

Finally I was there, outside the wolf park, which was, of course, closed for a two-hour lunch, as almost everything in rural France is – shops in some small towns even take three hours. But the sun was shining, so I sat on some rocks, spread out my picnic, and waited for opening time.

It was a truly memorable experience. The wolves were at liberty in a very large enclosure, apart from one or two in smaller pens close by for special reasons, usually medical, whilst we, the visitors, had to watch and observe them from the top of a stockade which was straight out of films like "The Alamo".

The guided tour was fascinating, full of information I didn't know, and easy to follow, as it was, of course, all in French. We watched the wolves being fed, then were told that if we made our way to a certain point we would be able to watch them go to drink and bathe, as they always liked to do so after eating.

Because I'd been there earlier than the other visitors, I'd already done a little recce of the lie of the land and spotted a real short-cut, down to the solid wooden palisade with glass panels inset, which enabled us to watch the wolves from very close up without disturbing them or putting ourselves in danger.

I stole away ahead of the rest of the party, got there first, and had several amazing minutes of being alone in the woods a few short feet away from a pack of European grey wolves, who were blissfully unaware of my presence and going about their ablutions as if they were unobserved.

Those were the good points and the highlights of my exploratory visit to the Limousin.

But what were the downsides which made me know beyond any doubt that this was not the region for me?

The scenery, for one thing. The bits I saw, admittedly probably not representative, were rather tame compared to the wild splendour of the Auvergne. There was not the dramatic sense of vastness and isolation I'd found there and loved.

Much of it was too similar to the parts of Wales I'd lived in, on and off, for fifteen years. And again it seemed to me pointless to move from one country to an almost identical region in another.

Then there was the Brit factor. In the Auvergne we hadn't seen or heard a single Brit. As soon as I landed at Limoges airport and walked out into the foyer, the first thing I saw was an English-speaking estate agent's stand. And I heard almost as much English as French spoken.

Worse, when I ordered a hot chocolate in the snack bar, there were Brits there making no effort at all to speak a single word of French to the French server, not even a merci when they received their order. One man even just pulled out a pawful of money and dropped it on the counter without making any attempt to select the right coins.

Now I'm dyscalculic. Only slightly, but enough to make me appear stupid with sums. And even I could work out that the round shiny thing exactly like a pound coin was a Euro, and the other coins had fifty, twenty, ten or five stamped on them to show how many centimes they represented. Not exactly rocket science.

I know, I'm too judgemental. I just knew that it wasn't for me. Back to dreams of the Auvergne.

# Part Four: When

As 2005 started to slip away towards the new year, we were all approaching something of a crossroads in our respective lives.

Although Mother was still quite content in the nice care home in the town where she was born and grew up – she used to tell everyone her father had built the row of houses opposite and he may well have done so, as he was a master builder working in that area – it was becoming clear that they were struggling to meet her needs in the way that they would like to.

She could no longer safely be encouraged to toddle about with her wheeled walking frame, in case she fell. It needed two of them to transfer her from room to room, even from chair to chair, she needed a lot of help and encouragement to eat and could no longer do anything much for herself. She still always knew who I was when I visited, and certainly knew who Meic was and welcomed him, but never me, with hugs and kisses.

I gave her an almost life-sized toy dog replica of him which she loved to have sitting on her bed, just to watch the startled expressions and nervous jumps from some of the carers when they came into her room and thought it was the real dog. To some extent she still retained her mischievous sense of humour.

It was getting harder to manage taking her out in the car, she took a bit of manhandling to get her in and out of it. But the home was right next to Taylor Park, so I would bundle her up in warm clothes if it was breezy and push her round in a wheelchair, with Meic trotting along beside, to look at the ducks on the pond, the flowers and trees and the occasional squirrel.

My brother was going through a particular period of discontent. It's debatable as to whether he has ever been truly happy in his life. Briefly so, perhaps, when he was first married, but that relationship ended fairly quickly, as did the engagement after that, as did a series of liaisons after that.

He had more or less taken up permanent residence at Mother's house, which was still standing idle since she first went into a home, and had decided to "do it up" with a view to letting. The quotation marks are because although in the past he had been very good at all aspects of DIY, as his drinking got worse, his skills slowly left him, as did his sense of proportion.

He would take on far too many, far too complex tasks and, instead of methodically finishing each then moving onto the next, he would start one, lose interest, start another, get stuck, start another and so on. So it reached the stage that not a single corner of a once beautifully kept and decorated house was habitable and most was stacked with all kinds of what other people would call junk, his, not Mother's.

Mother was a hoarder, but a hoarder with a very good eye, especially for antiques. She loved to watch the Antiques Roadshow and similar programmes, and had done an evening class in antiques. She loved finding treasures in charity shops or jumble sales, bringing them home and cleaning them up to find the true beauty, and value, hidden under years of dirt.

One of her best finds, of which she was particularly proud as she had found it at a jumble sale after the professional dealers had been through and cherry picked the best, was a fine early

Georgian silver bud vase. It had been blackened and filthy and she'd haggled to secure it for five pence. Once she'd cleaned it up and revealed its silver marks, it was probably worth at least fifty pounds.

My brother was just a hoarder, and he filled her house with all his stuff. One feature of bi-polar disorder can be a tendency towards wild spending sprees when on a high. Like buying a double-decker bus. And that followed on from owning a former black London cab and a vintage Rolls-Royce.

I'd once worked with a woman who had bi-polar disorder. She went out of the office one lunch time to go sales shopping for a pair of shoes she had seen and coveted and came back with fourteen pairs. It took two of us to help her carry all her purchases up the stairs to our office.

My brother always had an incredible quantity of clothing. When I finally helped him to start packing up his own house, I counted no fewer than one hundred and fifty shirts. And bear in mind that Mother's semi-detached house was quite small, so you can start to form a mental image of what it was looking like with a lot of his things in with Mother's collection of silver, china and scarves. Because she was a compulsive scarf collector and must have had at least as many scarves as my brother had shirts.

My brother had taken up residence at Mother's house as he'd had a fairly major fire in his own house in South Wales, the second he'd had there, which meant he'd lost a lot of his possessions. And this was something which affected him very deeply and awoke bad memories.

He stayed living in our parents' home for some time after I moved out, in the 1970s, while he tried to decide what direction to take his career in next. He'd had a go at printing and at electronics. Then he surprised us all by announcing he was joining the Royal Fleet Auxiliary as a ship's purser. This from someone who only had to watch newsreel of the cross channel ferry to get seasick.

When he went off to sea, he bundled all his possessions up and put them into the loft at our parents' house for safe-keeping and to be out of the way. The Aged Parent decided to throw them away. Without asking or telling him. I don't know why. It was just fairly typical of the way he was.

My brother was devastated. All his personal stuff, photographs, tape recordings of various long-dead family members, all sorts of irreplaceable things, chucked out with the rubbish. To my knowledge, my brother has never thrown anything away since, not even a newspaper.

If you were brave enough to open the door of his fridge at any time, I could guarantee you would find "fresh" fish dating back several years, which he'd bought, forgotten about and left to rot. Very sad, very tragic. And very annoying to someone like me who's always been frugal and can't bear waste of any description.

Around this time, in his increasing state of discontent, he'd started taking Italian lessons and opera singing lessons and talking about possibly going to live in Italy.

I'd finally succeeded in talking him out of the crazy idea of his ever bringing Mother's house up to the standard required to be able to let it and instead to put it on the market. This would give us one less thing to worry about, as well as freeing up some of Mother's capital to meet the spiralling costs of her care.

So as well as finding the time to visit Mother as often as possible, I was also having to go to her house and begin the not inconsiderable task of clearing it of years of clutter, hers and my brother's, putting her most precious antique furniture into storage, and generally making it marketable.

Meic was trundling gently along, still on his heart medication, still defying the vet's prognosis, still meeting the requirements of the Squeaky Toy Rule and looking like a dog who could possibly defeat the odds and make a new life for himself somewhere else.

And me? I was happy enough as I was. I loved my cottage, now promoted from grottage, with a lovely garden, all created by my own hands.

My predecessor there obviously had some very serious issues as, once I started digging in the mass of nettles and runaway lonicera nitida, which was all there was of a garden, all I came up with was endless pairs of tights stuffed inside Walkers' crisp packets. I'm not sure which flavour. The blue bags. I only like the plain ones so I don't know the colours of the different flavours.

But whatever the former resident had been trying to achieve, I can tell you that no matter what type of soil you plant that combination in, it simply doesn't grow into anything.

I loved my copywriting but had major crises of confidence of making it my full-time occupation. I was always aware of my age compared to all the young things out there, and the drawback of not reading all the fashion magazines and keeping up to date with the latest trends.

I'd spat my dummy from the chugger (charity mugger) job. I've done some grafting in my time – I've looked after more than twenty horses single handed on top of a Welsh mountain in the middle of nowhere in some pretty extreme weather, including minus twenty-five Celsius in the wind chill. But for sheer grinding you down, I would have to vote chugging as the hardest job I've ever done.

Many chuggers are paid, which the public often don't realise. The method differs from charity to charity, but in my case I was paid per person enrolled as a member of the Wildlife Trust I worked for. And that meant no new recruits, no pay for that shift.

Lincolnshire is a much bigger county than most people realise, with very few motorway miles. So our chuggers could drive up to two and a half hours each way to reach a destination such as a supermarket, shopping centre or garden centre.

The shifts were supposed to be six hours but as, at that time, there were only two of us chugging, neither of us in the first flush of youth, we drew the line at six hours on our feet, often outside in the car park, depending on the venue, in all weathers, and opted instead for five-hour shifts.

At some venues we were not even allowed to speak to the passing public, just stand there grinning inanely at them in the forlorn hope they might take pity and stop to talk to us.

Which they hardly ever did. The most we were ever allowed to do was to smile and say: "Can I interest you in the Wildlife Trust?"

We might pose the question two hundred or more times in a shift and if we succeeded in signing up four people, we'd had a good day. But on a bad day we could conceivably, and sometimes did, though not often, due to sheer dogged determination, drive five hours, stand five hours and head home knowing we had earned not a single penny for our efforts. And we weren't paid a mileage allowance.

I did it for nearly two years including, with my colleague, taking over all the work of finding and booking the venues, but at the end of that, I felt enough was enough.

I'd also had a teddy-throwing moment at the further education college where I'd taught riding and stable management and been a course tutor. It was getting harder and harder to teach, with the odds stacked more and more in favour of the students, and the lecturers not having any real authority.

It was no longer possible for students to fail. They had instead to be "referred" to repeat the work until it reached the required standards. So it became a game of me practically writing their assignments for them, then giving them a pass or even a merit which they hadn't really merited.

In addition, there were the constant complaints against members of staff by students, with the results going the wrong way and the pendulum swinging too far. A good friend and colleague had a complaint lodged against her for a totally heinous crime – she actually had the temerity to suggest her students should hand in their assignments. By the appointed date. How unreasonable!

Another who told a business studies student to take off his baseball cap in the classroom was told she did not have the right to do so. I was told I didn't have the right to tell my equine students to remove their body piercings before riding. Despite being responsible for their safety, as well as being the duty first aider in case of accident.

There was just one boy in my group amongst the females, sixteen years old, and newly come out of the closet, who delighted in telling us all about his intimate body piercings and reminding me I couldn't insist on their removal. He was quite a large lad, there were only two horses big enough to carry him and only really one suitable for his level of ability. It was amazing how often that horse was lame when I wrote the ride list, leaving him without a horse. Until he had a light-bulb moment and removed his piercings, whereupon the horse underwent an amazing recovery.

There was also the attitude of the management towards the part-time lecturers. Having run the equine course successfully for a year, with good results from my students, I was expected to spend time, unpaid, through the summer, recruiting for a course for the following year. Then to apply for the job I had already been doing and might possibly not get.

In addition, I would find myself being timetabled to go in for just an hour a day on some occasions, despite pointing out that an hour's pay barely covered my fuel to get there and asking for at least two hours at a time to make it worth my while. Life's too short. Move on.

So fate/karma/supreme being (delete/add as appropriate to your personal beliefs) was clearly giving us all a little nudge in a new direction.

When my brother was talking about heading for Italy, I suggested he take a look at prices in the Auvergne, and directed him to a particular website I'd been browsing where there was, amongst other properties, an auberge for sale.

He'd always been a good, if catastrophically messy, cook, used to large-scale catering, having been naval trained to feed a ship's company. So I was thinking that if perhaps he could revive an interest in cooking he might just manage to turn himself around and sort his life out.

He was hugely enthusiastic about the prospect of an auberge and immediately started making plans to go and view it. I must have been at a particularly low ebb that day since I found myself saying: "If you get it, I'll come and run the B&B side of it for you."

Now it has to be said that my brother and I have never been particularly close. In fact, saying that is rather on a par with saying Imelda Marcos had quite a few pairs of shoes. We're usually best off when not breathing the same air.

But I don't like to see any soul in such evident torment. And as I was often having to chase round after him dealing with his latest catastrophe, it occurred to me that it might make sense to have him close enough to keep an eye on, in the hopes that that would help.

So then what about Mother? There were then no cheap flights (minya, minya, minya, key change) from Clermont to anywhere useful to us and anyway neither of us flew from choice, so popping over for the weekend was going to be out of the question.

Lightbulb moment – what if we found a property that was large enough and suitable to house all of us, Mother, Brother, Meic and me?

Which is why January 2006 found my brother and me boarding the Eurostar for a property-viewing trip to the Auvergne.

My brother loves travelling by train, and loves staying in hotels, so even if we didn't find a suitable property, it would make a nice break for him, with some company. And he clearly intended to have a good time since he was drinking his first beer of the day in London at nine o'clock in the morning.

He then went off for a Brief Encounter moment with one of the many women he dated through internet sites. He'd recently had a dalliance with a truly stunning looking young Russian woman. I kept think of the later series of "Auf Wiedersehen,

Pet", and Barry's Russian wife Tatiana. It seems this one wasn't as desperate for a British passport, though, as the liaison soon fizzled out.

We had a pleasant and uneventful journey down to Clermont-Ferrand and a taxi to our hotel, all ready to collect our hire car and begin the serious business of house-hunting.

French estate agents in this region are fiercely protective of their properties. They absolutely will not allow you to go and look at them unless they accompany you. You won't find property addresses or instructions of where to find the house on any of their property details, which tend to be sketchy.

We preferred to go and have at least a look at the outside of a place on our own first to see if it's worth making an appointment to view the interior, and sometimes the location alone can be enough to put us off.

The Auberge du Piarrou was easy to find. Not far outside Thiers and well sign-posted, so it must, in its day, have been something of note. It had clearly fallen on hard times latterly, though, as it looked run-down and long closed. But the location was good, the signposts were in place and it looked a possibility, so we mentally ticked it off for an internal visit, and went off into Thiers for lunch and to confirm a viewing with the agent.

We were about to learn a very important lesson about French property purchase. What you see is definitely not always what you get. What the online details and photographs didn't make clear was that not all of the building formed part of the sale.

Fair enough. But in strange Auvergnat fashion, the building was not simply split in two from top to bottom nor even from side to side, but rather in a zigzag fashion like a course of bricks. So a room that jutted into the auberge actually belonged to the neighbour and vice versa. Also the very smart professional kitchen which had so impressed my brother on the website had been stripped out and sold separately, with no apparent reduction in the price.

That'll be a non, then.

From Thiers we drove on further south in the Livradois-Forez to the small town of Arlanc to meet up again with the same agent who'd shown us round the auberge, and look round a maison de maître (gentleman's residence). It was certainly a large and imposing building, on a fairly quiet main road, with a lovely walled garden and something clearly no French gentleman can live without – a princess tower.

The agent explained that the merchant who built the house had a very spoilt daughter who always got exactly what she wanted. And she wanted a princess tower. In pink. So he had one made, on the side of the house. About four storeys high, with a precarious viewing platform at the top and absolutely no practical function at all.

My brother was quite brave, as he's also acrophobic, and actually managed to step out onto the platform. My rubbery legs took me to the top of all the stairs but no further.

The ground floor was let as a doctor's surgery – handy for house calls for Mother – and there were lots of rooms for doing B&B, since we were thinking of a possible income-generating sideline. But the town was incredibly quiet, and checking on the various tourist activities in the area, like the panoramic railway, the window for attracting tourists and making money out of them was perilously short.

Merci, but non, merci.

The agent wasn't done with us yet, though, and she certainly had vision. We'd said we didn't mind something that needed a little work, as long as there was somewhere safe and suitable for Mother in the meantime.

Her next offering was an enormous, derelict former factory at Courpière. Right. Erm, we seem to have lost something in the translation here. As loading bays go, it was quite a pleasant one, but perhaps not quite what we had in mind for accommodating a, by now, nearly ninety-year-old mother.

Next...

Ridiculous to sublime perhaps best describes her next offering. A three-storey house in a very quiet hamlet with a wonderful large covered verandah on the first floor, amazing oak beams and carvings everywhere, all recently done, and, on the ground floor, or lower ground floor correctly speaking, as it was built on the side of a hill, a self-contained apartment, with its own hammam. Every house should have one.

I could see that my brother was very tempted. It had the possibility of working for all our requirements. It needed very little work and the apartment would have been perfect for Mother, with its own bathroom all on one level. I also knew it was right at the upper limit, or perhaps beyond, the budget my brother had set himself, as he was buying the house, and he had yet to put his own property on the market, let alone sell it. I dragged him away before he could do anything rash without discussing it.

The next day we ventured further north into the Allier département and tried another agent, with the idea of covering all bases. We looked first at a roadside bar/restaurant which was still trading and seemed to get busy.

My brother was keen. It was on a busy road for passing trade. To me it was a nightmare. So much traffic, not enough peace and tranquillity and I couldn't see it being very enjoyable for Mother being taken for little walks alongside a busy road with all the traffic fumes. Also, as she was deaf and wore a hearing aid, the noise of the traffic would have been painful for her every time I took her out, and she did love her little trips out.

Next...

Further west to one of France's Most Beautiful Villages, Charroux. Although for me it didn't compare with the ones I'd seen down in the Cantal. It was a strange place, on a little low plateau with nothing much in the way of views. And although the town itself was quaint and quirky, with its little narrow twisty roads, it had a bit of a claustrophobic feel about it.

The house was huge and rambling, again with tons of potential, but also in need of much more work than the agent had led us to believe.

And another one bites the dust.

As an aside here, a word of warning to property hunters making their first foray to France. It's a lot bigger than England! It seems such a basic statement. But the number of Brits who fail to realise the distances involved getting from A to B, often on slow twisty roads, is incredible.

Those who plan their own itinerary often seriously under-estimate the time it takes to get from property to property. Those who arrange to be driven about by a French estate agent need to ensure they have nerves of steel, a liberal supply of Valium and preferably a change of underwear, rural French driving being what it is.

Don't worry, if you opt to drive yourself, that you may forget which side of the road to drive on, though. In the Auvergne, the correct side is exactly in the middle, which is where everyone drives. In fact you can spot a Brit a mile away, although they are still quite thin on the ground. They'll be the ones driving on the right - the big sissies.

And as for roundabouts and the rules over signalling, there are two rules of the road in the Auvergne to cover those modern inconveniences. Either don't signal at all, as everyone should know where you're going. Or lie. That will keep other drivers on their toes.

We were getting very close to the end of our stay and I know my brother was itching to achieve something, to be able to go back and tell Mother he had bought a house where she could live with us and be looked after.

He was very keen on the house with the hammam. I liked the house, it ticked all our boxes, Mother would love it, especially the covered terrace, if we put in a stair lift to get her up to it, and it was ready to move into.

My big concern was that he would be over-stretching himself financially. He was retired, had been for years on health grounds, on a reasonable, although not excessive, pension. Also he had recently had his rambling ruin in Wales valued by a local estate agent for more than twice what I expected and what I personally thought it was worth or would realise, although I'm not an estate agent.

We talked it over at dinner and agreed to go back the next day for another look and consider the options. It was a snowy day and it all looked very pretty. I took my eye off the ball for a nano-second to look at the garden and came back to find my brother and the agent shaking hands on an offer he had made which had been accepted.

And so back to the UK to put things into motion to make it happen, which would involve selling his house, finalising the sale of Mother's house, letting my house and finding a suitable means of transporting an elderly person with various health concerns a thousand miles to start a new life in a new country.

* * *

My brother has a theory that some sort of curse haunts our family, which turns all things to worms in short order. It's true that he, in particular, has been known to snatch defeat from the jaws of victory on more than one occasion.

I don't think we're necessarily any more cursed than any other family. We certainly haven't been visited by many real tragedies. Things go wrong, but that's just life. As they say, shit happens – get over it.

But I suppose it wasn't entirely unexpected that shortly after our triumphant return from France, with pictures of our proposed new home to wave at all and sundry, the wheels started to come off the entire venture.

Once paperwork started to be exchanged, we noticed that the vendor hadn't included all of the garden which we had seen in the sale. He wanted to keep back a parcel of land, close to the house, to build another house. It put an entirely different complexion on the whole affair, as part of the attraction was that it was a detached house with plenty of room all round.

The garden as we were shown it was a good size for Meic to totter about in, and for Mother to be wheeled into a different place each day so she would feel she was having lots of different adventures and picnics. It also meant it was going to be quiet, with no immediate neighbour noise and no need to worry about things like having to have the television on at white noise level for Mother to hear.

So my brother just rather took his foot off the gas pedal and let the deal slip away. It was a shame – we'd both loved the large covered balcony and the idea of having a hamman in the basement.

But our little trip to France had whetted his appetite for the whole idea. So he proposed another foray to find something else, which was duly booked for May, 2006.

Once again we found ourselves boarding the Eurostar, this time having managed to wangle a last-minute upgrade, which meant that all meals and drinks were free. Needless to say, my brother wasn't going to let any of the free alcohol go to waste.

This time we'd picked out some possible properties for ourselves from the internet and made an appointment to see an English estate agent south of Clermont-Ferrand.

We didn't particularly seek out English estate agents, we chose this one simply because she had some of the properties that interested us on her books. Both of us speak enough French to get by in most situations, though of course, like any non-native speakers of a language, we drop the occasional clanger and make fools of ourselves.

My brother worked for some time in Brussels, speaking French and Flemish, and as his job involved writing a lot of official paperwork in French, his written French is good in terms of construction. Sometimes his accent lets him down a little, although he blames that on a tendency to speak French with a Belgian accent.

When speaking French, I'm often asked where I'm from, since most people can immediately identify that I'm not French but don't seem to pick up on my English roots. I'm often asked if I'm Dutch, although I'm a good six inches too short, so can only assume my accent and sentence construction has been influenced by speaking French with the Luxembourg family.

I'm the first to throw up my hands and admit to speaking French "comme une vache espagnole" as the French say, although why a Spanish cow would be speaking French at all, let alone with a poor accent, is beyond me.

My brother is reluctant to accept that his accent might possibly be at all to blame for misunderstandings. He just always assumes the person to whom he is speaking must be a moron, if he is not understood.

There was one memorable occasion as we dined in an hotel in Clermont and he was wanting to impress the waiter by telling him he spoke "russe" which is French for Russian.

The French "u" is difficult for the Anglo-Saxon tongue to pronounce as it doesn't really have an equivalent. The nearest is probably "ew". The "ou" sound is much easier as it is more like the English "oo". So my brother was actually saying he spoke "rousse". Which is French for red-head, not "russe" which is French for Russian. You can see why the waiter was confused. He'd clearly never met a fluent speaker of red-head before.

The agent we had arranged to see was based a bit further south than Clermont-Ferrand and she recommended an hotel at Issoire which seemed very good value, although my brother was disappointed that it didn't have a bar or restaurant. We were assured that there was a good auberge just a short walk down the road, so he agreed to book the hotel.

When we arrived by train to Issoire, we didn't really know how far the station was from the hotel and there were no signs of any taxis anywhere. I asked a woman, who was collecting a passenger, for directions, and we discovered how incredibly kind the Auvergnats can be. Although it was out of her way and her car was already well laden, she somehow managed to shoe-horn both of us and our cases into her little car and drive us to the door of a clean, modern hotel.

We collected another hire car the next morning and set off to find the agent. Having learned our lessons from the last trip, we were very explicit in what we needed this time and confident that with an English agent there should be no possibility at all of anything getting lost in translation.

We specified a large enough house for the three of us to co-habit without being on top of one another, a good sized garden, as Mother loved flowers and birds and sitting outside, not too isolated, with a railway station or bus stop within walking distance for my brother, and well enough appointed that we could realistically move straight in with a frail elderly lady in tow.

We were pleased that she did seem to grasp what we were looking for, as when we mentioned one of her properties which we'd seen on the website she said she would not even take us to see if as it was so unsuitable for mother's needs it would simply not be worth the effort to view it.

She certainly seemed to have hoisted in most of our points, as the first house was very nice, ticked almost all of the boxes and had distinct possibilities for us. It was also a very attractive price, considerably less than the house with the hammam. It went onto the short list.

We couldn't fault her on the second one, either. It had a superb mature garden Mother would have loved and was in very reasonable condition and decorative order. Just for some reason neither of us took to it. It had a bit of a "so what" factor.

House number three was gorgeous, with absolutely stunning views. Except it was miles from anywhere and with a road up to it which, for winter, would have required a team of huskies instead of an elderly border collie. And the walking distance to a railway station would have given a paratrooper pause for thought.

And number four was just scruffy. A big old house, in the middle of a village, lots of room, but very run down and looked in need of a good bottoming, as Mother would say. The décor was very hippy chic. And it has to be said that solid blocks of turquoise, orange and purple paint are not to everyone's taste and would probably have given Mother a migraine.

The following day was going to have to be a day off from house-hunting as we'd quite forgotten the importance of Ascension Day, a bank holiday, in France and all the agents were likely to be closed. Instead we walked into Issoire and watched in amazement as council workers with big machines came and shampooed the town square and surrounding streets, then jet washed them to rinse.

We had planned a trip further south, to Aurillac, the next day, near to a place my brother had visited with his Russian girlfriend and her sister, who apparently always chaperoned her on their encounters. But a phone call at one o'clock in the morning from my brother's room put paid to that – he was ill.

I called reception who kindly called the duty doctor who called an ambulance, which took the two of us off to hospital in Issoire. This was my first direct experience of the French health care system and I was very impressed.

Without going into too much detail for the squeamish amongst you, my brother was having something of a plumbing crisis. He was seen, diagnosed, treated, medicated, given an out-patient appointment and discharged, all within the space of two hours, by a doctor who spoke fluent English, had we needed that additional service. But after such a late night, neither of us felt much like a long car journey that day.

Instead we went into Issoire and found another estate agent we hadn't seen before, to whom we carefully laid out our requirements, and who then took us off to see a nearby house which had a very nice garden. But we would have needed a block and tackle to get Mother's wheelchair up and down the slope and the only access was through the garage and up some steep steps.

Perfect – not.

He then asked the rather bizarre question of whether we liked water. Rather guardedly we said yes, in the right context. He said he would take us to a house with an intriguing water feature, so we followed his car to a nearby small town where he led us to an amazing property with a large garden almost like a formal park. And the water feature turned out to be something rather like a mill race running through the middle of the garden.

He explained that he didn't actually have immediate access to the house but could arrange it if we liked what we saw. We did. It was in the middle of a small town, very like the one where my brother lived in Wales, but the big footprint of the garden made it feel a little detached from the traffic and noise.

There were all amenities close by, a bar opposite for my brother, a boulangerie just up the road and a very short walk away over a river bridge, open fields for me and Meic to walk. A definite positive. Although my brother was worried by the lack of light. He is prone to depression, especially to SAD (seasonal affective disorder) and was concerned about the somewhat gloomy aspect of the interior.

Our intrepid agent then said he had yet more to offer us and would lead us to our next viewing. He proceeded to floor the accelerator and burn rubber, disappearing towards the motorway with absolutely no use whatsoever of those pretty little flashing orange lights which cars have, another modern invention the Auvergnats tend to have no truck with.

Whilst I drove as fast and furiously as I could in the agent's wake, my brother attempted to call him on his mobile for at least a clue as to which way he had gone. Straight to voicemail. So we gave up and instead went to explore the beautiful nearby village of Usson, where we climbed a very steep hill to find the inevitable statue of the blessed virgin and enjoy the amazing views.

The next day we took the initiative and went back for another peek at the mill-race house by ourselves, and as chance would have it, met the owner coming out of the back garden gate. She was absolutely thrilled and said it had always been her dream to pass on her beautiful garden to some English people, as many of the French are convinced that all English are wonderful gardeners!

She apologised for not being able to show us round there and then but we made an appointment for the following day and went off for a little further exploration of our own, unconstrained by estate agents.

We'd managed to prise from one agent the name of the village where one of our choices from the internet was situated. Internet research showed the village had a population of only around three hundred and fifty, so armed with the internet print-out with a picture of the house, we went there and waved it at the first person we saw, who was able to direct us up to the top of the village, where we found the house.

Both on paper and in the flesh, so to speak, this one looked very promising. According to the internet details, it had seven bedrooms and three bathrooms, was on three storeys and had a good-sized garden. We nicknamed it the pink house, as the photo showed the rendering as a pale rose pink, although in reality it was a lot paler and more washed out.

It was built on a slope, so the garage and cellars were underneath the main house, with a small one-bedroom apartment on the ground floor. We liked the look of it. We discovered a decent small town just three kilometres away, on a bus route, and another much larger town, with a mainline railway station and all facilities, about nine kilometres away.

Tick, tick and tick again.

The following day, we went back for our appointment with the owner of the millrace house and found the estate agent there! That's how eager French agents are to earn their commission, as it was a Sunday. And who can blame them, as in France, both vendor and purchaser pay a percentage of the purchase price to the estate agent in commission.

We found another not uncommon feature of older French properties – the house was a back to back semi-detached. Plus side - lower heating bills. Minus side - much less daylight. The garden was truly a delight, though, and the big bonus was that it was already completely dog proof. It stayed high on the list of possibles.

We went for a run-out after that, westward to the Monts Dores then back via the Puy de Dôme and finally found the navette (shuttle bus) running, so took the stomach-churning ride to the summit for the incredible views.

*After the white knuckle ride to the summit, posing on the edge of the Puy de Dome, at 1464m, was a walk in the park for my brother.*

The journey up certainly rattled my brother, so he decided he couldn't possibly face the return journey on the navette. There is a pedestrian route up the Puy, an old mule track, but it brings you down to a car park a long walk from where we had left the hire car, near to the navette car park.

The direct route down to the navette car park is prohibited to pedestrians. The road is too narrow for more than one vehicle to pass at a time, so the navette drivers use what the French call talky-walkies to synchronise their departures from either end, so they only meet where there are designated passing places. And despite the steep gradient and plunging drop to the side, they rattle up and down as if they were in the Monte Carlo rally. Any pedestrian in their way would be toast, in very short order.

Trying to take any sort of short cut meant an extremely steep and slippery climb down and as it was a warm day, I had on my feet only my old, much-worn walking sandals with the tread worn down and not enough grip. Also, even though it was sunny and fine, we were still at 1,465 metres and I despise people who go walking in any sort of high country without provisions. We didn't have so much as a bottle of water. My normal minimum back pack contains food, water, space blanket, bivvy bag, compass and snake bite pump. So I dug my heels in and said it was the shuttle or nothing.

I hadn't enjoyed the trip up much, either. I'm a nervous passenger, I don't easily trust another driver. I'm the same flying. I would prefer to interview the pilot first to ensure he is happily married, with an accommodating mistress, pleased with the progress of his children at an affordable private school, up to date with his mortgage payments and not under undue stress of any kind. Entrusting my life to a French driver at the best of times is tricky – on that slope it was very difficult.

For most of the journey down, I had my eyes closed, so was pleased we'd been able to see the view from the top, as I certainly didn't see any of it on the way down.

On the way back towards our hotel, and armed with various computer printouts from estate agents' websites, we went for a look round for anything else suitable. Most that we were able to find were too isolated to be practical, or the access was no good for Mother in a wheelchair or on one occasion, seemed to consist of just a pile of old stones in the corner of a field. Improvable. So there was a lot riding on the following day's appointment with the agent to view the pink house.

They do warn house viewers to try to see past existing décor to what the place will look like once you've stamped your own mark on it. Sound advice. The decoration in the pink house was truly hideous. Very 1970s. The sitting room had two very strong contrasting patterned wallpapers, which didn't go together, neither of which was very nice even in isolation and in unison presented a full frontal assault to the senses.

But the layout was practically perfect for what we wanted. On the top floor was a bright, light three-bedroomed apartment with shower room and loo and some open space to create a small cooking and dining area. Ideal to let as B&Bs or a self-contained flat. It had very nice south-facing views, and the possibility to create a sunny roof terrace on top of the roof of the room below, which jutted out in front of it.

The middle floor had three good sized bedrooms, a bathroom and separate toilet, a reasonable sized kitchen and a spacious L-shaped dining room/sitting room. Or if you prefer, lounge/diner. I don't prefer, as lounge is a word I absolutely loathe. I'm probably a huge snob, and don't truly care, but I just find it a particularly ugly word, so prefer to stick to sitting room.

On the lower ground floor, since the middle storey was at ground level on two sides because of the slope, was a small apartment with a kitchen, bedroom and shower room. Ideal for my brother as, although he would be the owner of the house so could choose the best of the bedrooms for himself, he is so pathologically untidy even he admitted it would be better to try to confine himself to a small area to avoid spreading chaos throughout the house. There was also a two-car garage, a laundry and a couple of cellar rooms.

The garden was effectively on three levels. The sitting room opened out onto a south-facing patio, set well up above the road so not overlooked, with a triangular shaped lawn to the side running up to a point at the top of the garden.

In front of the lower floor apartment was parking for at least another three cars, a reasonable sized vegetable patch and several espaliered apple and pear trees, with a mature plum tree at the end of the row.

*It wasn't as pink as the online images had led us to believe, but the "pink house" was the most promising of all those we had seen so far.*

From the kitchen garden, concrete steps led down to a small enclosed meadow about twenty metres by fifteen meters, with three mirabelle plum trees and another mature plum, plus what had clearly been an old poultry house. What's more, the whole package was a good chunk less than the hammam house had been.

This time I managed to drag my brother away to discuss it further before he had time to do anything rash, urging him that we should look at a few more houses before reaching a final decision.

We went off to explore in more detail the nearby largish town of Riom. And we had a chuckle on the way with the name of the town. Almost always, I drove while my brother map-read, which suited us both best.

Roads numbers in France are prefixed by a letter, N for national, D for départemental. We came to a large roundabout and my brother pointed towards an exit and said: "That's the road we need, the R-ten-M." It was such an unfamiliar format for a road number that I wavered, missed the exit and carried on round the roundabout to try again.

And saw the sign for myself. Er, that'll be RIOM, then, on the D2144!

We spent a long time talking to yet another estate agent and setting out our list of requirements. He was a pleasant young man, keen as mustard but obviously hadn't listened to a word we'd said and had his own agenda.

The first property he showed us, near Manzat, needed a lot of work. If we hadn't liked the front door there would have been no problem – the large crack in the outside wall was so wide that any of the three of us, none of us being terribly bulky of build, could have walked through it sideways.

For the second property, he led us in convoy down the A89 motorway, on which we drove. And drove. And drove. In fact we thought we must be almost into the Limousin by the time we reached our destination. But it has to be said the A89 is a lovely motorway on which to drive, with its views of the volcanoes and the Massif du Sancy. It's also the quietest motorway we'd ever seen, with an incredibly low volume of traffic.

The property we'd travelled all that way to see was remarkable. It was pleasant from the outside, with a steep slate roof, and a veritable Tardis on the inside. Every door the agent opened seemed to reveal yet another huge attic space crying out to be converted into accommodation. The price was incredible, too, by far the cheapest of comparable size we'd seen on any of our trips.

So there had to be a downside. The first red flag was the shared access driveway with the neighbouring property. Great if you get on, nightmare if things go wrong with the entente cordiale. Plus it was miles from anywhere, not very practical for B&B customers who'd struggle to find it, with not much to bring them to the area in the first place.

Then there was the surrounding countryside. As my brother pointed out, we were a long way from the volcanoes and volcanic mountain peaks that make the area so dramatically beautiful. We were into tame, low-lying countryside, lightly wooded, which could quite easily have been rural Cheshire. A bit pointless to uproot and settle in an area that looked exactly like the one in which we both grew up.

Nuh-nur, as they say in Family Fortunes.

We again took the scenic route back to the hotel via Le Mont Dore for a closer look at the Puy de Sancy, at 1,886 metres, the highest point of the Massif Central and therefore the highest peak in central France. We were above the snowline in many places and the stunning and dramatic views convinced us that if we were making this sea-change, it should be to somewhere which at least had a sight of all this dramatic beauty.

So the next day we drove into Clermont to the agent's, where my brother put in an offer at the asking price on the pink house, which was accepted. Déja-vu?

And once more we were on our way back to the UK via Eurostar, armed with pictures of a possible future house to show to Mother and anyone else who might be interested.

How different the UK was starting to look after these trips to France, and to the wide open spaces of the Auvergne in particular. London looked dirty, crowded and depressing. We paused for an expensive cup of tea in a station coffee bar which tried to rip me off over the price charged.

We arrived early at the station and were told at the ticket office that we could take an earlier train than the one booked. We ran like mad things, hauling our cases, only to be turned back at the barrier by an unhelpful Jobsworth who disagreed with his colleague and said we could only get onto the train we were booked on, not the one about to depart, even though it was clearly not full.We said very rude things to each other about him and his ancestry in French by way of revenge. But we were back. An offer had been accepted. Mission was accomplished. We hoped.

# Part Five: How

Have you ever played fox, chicken, corn, river? You know the one: you have to get a fox, a chicken, and a sack of corn across a river. You have a rowing boat, but it can only carry you and one other thing. If the fox and the chicken are left together, the fox will eat the chicken. If the chicken and the corn are left together, the chicken will eat the corn. How do you get them all safely to the other side?

In the flush of success, we hadn't really realised that trying to synchronise the move, possibly permanent, of three of us (not forgetting Meic the dog) from three separate and not particularly close locations in the UK to one destination in France was going to be rather a similar puzzle.

But first there was the purchase of the French house to be completed, and the disposal of three UK properties to be seen to.

My little cottage in Lincolnshire was going to be the easiest of the three to sort out. The postcode was very desirable and it was such a small hamlet that properties very rarely came on the market. I'd done a lot of work on it and it was very nice, even though I say so myself. I wanted initially to let it, so I would still have a toehold in the UK should the French venture go disastrously wrong, but I also wanted a rough idea of its market value should I decide to sell, or fail to find a tenant.

I called two estate agents to come and give their opinion. The first was from a local firm specialising in rural properties. He greeted Meic enthusiastically almost before he acknowledged me and said what a lovely sitting room it was. The second ignored Meic, grumbled about dog hairs and said the lounge was a good size.

Guess which one I picked?

French property sales can sometimes, though not always, go through surprisingly swiftly and smoothly. As my brother wasn't relying on the sale of his Welsh property to go ahead with the purchase in France, we had a provisional date of the beginning of December 2006 to think about making the move.

My newly-appointed estate agent turned out to be amazingly efficient and found me a tenant with excellent references, all eager and ready to move in on the thirty-first of August.

This gave me a huge dilemma. Take what seemed to be a very good, very reliable tenant and effectively make myself homeless or say no and hope the agent could find me someone again later in the year when the move to France looked more imminent.

Mother, meanwhile, was yo-yoing between the home and hospital as she continued to have episodes which worried the care home. They were often TIAs – mini-strokes – but the concern with those is that they are often an early warning of worse to come. The home was brilliant with her, we really had no complaints at all, just the odd minor niggle, inevitably, but it was not a nursing home and was not equipped to cope with the kind of medical supervision someone of Mother's age and infirmity needed.

We were also starting to think about the practicalities of getting the contents of three houses out to France. There was plenty of room in the pink house for virtually everything we wanted to take with us, but we would still have to collect it all up from three locations and get it out there.

Mother had collected a lot of antique furniture, and especially china and silver, over the years. I felt it might be the time to sell it, rather than have the cost of storing and transporting it. Most of it was English, so if we wanted to sell it at a later date once we'd got to France we might struggle to find a market for its style. Needless to say my brother, the inveterate hoarder, wanted to keep it. So the only option was to put it into storage while we attempted to sell her house, ready to ship to France at a later date.

We looked into the cost of removals, both hiring a professional company and hiring a lorry to do it ourselves. In the end my brother decided the way forward, with three houses to clear, would be to buy a furniture van and do it all ourselves. Like you do.

I wasn't unduly concerned, since we are both grafters, not afraid of hard physical work. Also a furniture van was the size of the large horse boxes I was used to driving, including all over Germany and back from there to the UK. We went to look at one in Manchester and he bought it.

My brother was full of confidence about driving it himself as, if you remember, he was the proud owner of a Leyland Routemaster bus ("hold very tight please – ting-ting", if you're old enough to remember the Flanders and Swann song.)

But it has to be said that this particular old van had a bit of a mind of its own. It was under the HGV limit – just – but had very stiff gears, so I almost had to stand upright on the clutch to shift gears, and the brakes were a bit of a law unto themselves. Too light on the pedal and you found yourself bowling on rather alarmingly long past the point where you wanted to stop. Too heavy and you had to peel yourself off the windscreen like a squashed bug.

Although my brother did drive it, he became increasingly nervous in doing so. So when eventually we came to take it, fully laden with stuff from my house and boxes from his house in Wales, up to the off-road storage place in Hereford where he kept his bus, with it wallowing like an old walrus with probably too much weight stacked too high up, he was reduced to driving at considerably less than twenty miles per hour on country lanes where it was very difficult for the irate procession of drivers stuck behind us to overtake.

By now Mother's house had been sold. All her precious furniture was safely in storage. And I'd taken what I thought would have been an unthinkable decision to move into my brother's house so I could go ahead with letting my own to what looked being very promising tenants, a very nice young couple with excellent reference.

Well, I thought to myself, it won't be for long, we'll soon be in France and things will start to look up.

Cock-eyed optimism, remember?

To be fair, it can't have been any easier a prospect for my brother. It's one thing to lie in emails saying you're doing wonderfully, cleaning and tidying up the house is going well and you haven't had a drink for weeks. Having someone living under the same roof and able to see for themselves how far from the truth this was would present him with difficulties.

And snatching defeat from the jaws of victory, remember? The purchase of the pink house was not going altogether swimmingly. My brother tends to take life rather too personally. Everyday annoyances which we all face and overcome, he sees as further evidence of the curse which he alleges dogs the family.

He was taking out a French mortgage to part-fund the pink house purchase. When the French bank wanted to see evidence of his income and outgoings for the past few months, he was absolutely outraged, as if it was some personal violation. Useless me pointing out everyone else did the same, I'd done so myself for the mortgage on my little Lincolnshire cottage.

The early warning signs that my moving in with him was not going to be easy for either of us started some five days before my new tenants were due to move in. My brother had said he would drive the lorry up to my house to collect all my furniture and take it to the off-road storage at Hereford.

The morning of the day this was due to happen, he phoned me to say he would not be able to come as he "wasn't well". Even at nearly three hundred miles apart and without a medical degree, it was easy to diagnose over the phone what the nature of his "illness" was.

As a precaution, he'd taken himself off to hospital and got himself admitted overnight. They were used to him at his local hospital, where he was a fairly frequent visitor. And whenever he was anxious for an alibi to show he was ill, not drunk, he would take himself there. It's so he can quote Spike Milligan's epitaph: "I told you I was ill."

Panic was starting to set in. My house was fully furnished still. I needed to get it emptied and myself moved out and I had very little time to do it in. I insisted my brother come up with a Plan B from his sick-bed, since everything so far had been riding on his Plan A, now out of the window. He did manage to rally himself sufficiently to find a Lincolnshire furniture remover and get him to phone me.

A nail-biting couple of days followed, since the removals man was not free until the day before my tenants were due to move in and I was not happy that the Plan B didn't have its own Plan B. But there was simply nothing else I could do since, it seems, rather a lot of people were moving house at the end of August and there simply wasn't anyone else available.

Moving day dawned and, true to their word, the removers were there in good time that afternoon as promised and made a quick and efficient job of clearing and loading all my worldly goods into their van.

They were to deliver to Wales on the following afternoon. My brother had at least managed to get his furniture van as far as the car park opposite his house and my goods were to be loaded onto that, with any remaining space being filled with whatever he could get at from his house.

In the meantime, what of Mother? Since our return from France, a few short weeks before, she had had two further admissions to hospital where we'd been very disconcerted by the poor level of care she had received. Whilst understanding the severe problems of staffing levels on wards, we were very worried that nobody seemed to be available to help Mother to eat, which she was incapable of doing unassisted, and she was losing a lot of weight.

The hospital's PALS (Patient Advice and Liaison Service) were very kind and helpful and did what they could to help. We pointed out that we both lived too far away to make daily visits to feed Mother. One of their representatives met me on the ward to see what they could do.

We found Mother sitting in front of a bowl of what might have been soup of some description but looked as if it would very effectively creosote a garden shed, and a sandwich so thick it would have taken the jaws of a crocodile to encompass. Even if they had appeared even remotely appetising, they were placed outside Mother's reach.

The PALS representative said straight away she could see what the problem was and said to Mother: "That doesn't look very appetising, does it?"

Mother leaned across to her and said in a confidential tone: "To be honest, it isn't really my sort of food."

Clearly, as frail as she was becoming, she wouldn't be able to go back to a straightforward care home, she was increasingly in need of the next level up, full-time nursing care. And as I was now going to be living with my brother in South Wales for the time being, we decided the best course of action would be to find a nursing home or a care home with nursing facilities in that area, where it would be easy for us to visit her daily, prior to our move to France.

I had the job of telling all the very kind staff of the lovely care home in St Helens, who had become very fond of Mother, and of Meic, that we would be taking her away. I explained our reasons, which they accepted. I also told them we were planning to take Mother to France to start a new life. They thought we were stark staring bonkers and she would never last the journey, never mind enjoy any of her new life if we ever got her to the other side of the channel.

Mother was by this time nearly ninety years old. Her various diagnosed ailments included vascular dementia, a leaking mitral heart valve, angina, myeloma, osteoporosis, Dupuytren's contracture of the left hand (where the fingers were permanently closed into a fist) osteoarthritis and a hiatus hernia. She could only totter a few steps, with maximum assistance and a wheeled walking frame.

But she still got a lot of enjoyment out of life. She loved her picnics and going out to parks and garden centres. She enjoyed her food, when someone helped her to eat it. Her eyesight was still as sharp as anything and although she was quite deaf, she could still follow her favourite television programmes like Bargain Hunt, Cash in the Attic and To Buy or Not To Buy, with the sub-titles on.

Her eyesight was truly amazingly good, and she could spot a speck of dust on a piece of furniture from yards away, since she had always been incredibly house-proud and kept her own little home immaculate. It was a measure of how good the care home was that she never found fault with their house-keeping.

She loved having tea parties and being the centre of attention, though only in small groups as she tended to get confused if there were too many people about, especially as her deafness made it difficult for her to follow conversations.

She could still recite a lot of the poems she had learned as a child. She could no longer make conversation, as such, so whenever there was a quiet moment which she felt the need to fill, she would trot out her two favourites, "The Witch" and "Where Are the Snowdrops", which she did several times a day.

Neither is particularly well known so I'll share them with
you:

The Witch

I saw her picking cowslips<br>
And marked her where she stood.<br>
She never knew I watched her<br>
Whilst hiding in the wood.

Her skirt was brightest crimson<br>
And black her steeple hat.<br>
Her broomstick lay beside her,<br>
I'm very sure of that.

Her chin was sharp and pointed,<br>
Her eyes, I don't know.<br>
For when she turned towards me,<br>
I thought it best to go.

*Percy H. Ilott*

Which she always delivered with great theatrical gesture, a
pregnant pause after "towards me" and a whispered last line.
And:

Where are the Snowdrops?

"Where are the snowdrops?" said the sun<br>
"Dead," said the frost,<br>
"Buried and lost<br>
Every one."

"A foolish answer," said the sun<br>
"They did not die,

130

Asleep they lie
Every one.

And I will awake them
I, the sun, into the light
All clad in white
Every one."

*Author unknown but possibly Annie Matheson (1853-1924)*

I can't find it anywhere else in any other literary reference, but Mother always added another verse to "Where Are the Snowdrops". It's in a completely different style and metre and I have a suspicion that it may possibly have been added by some long-forgotten school teacher who felt the ending was a little abrupt otherwise:

So they struggled and toiled, by day and by night,
Till two little snowdrops in green and white,
Rose out of the darkness and into the light,
And softly kissed one another.

\* \* \*

As one of his business ventures, my brother had run a private ambulance service and had had some experience of delivering elderly patients to various care homes in his surrounding area.

It's just possible that he had been pre-programmed from a very early age to become 'Peter of the Ambulance', since another of mother's favourite rhymes was a song about Peasley Cross, one of the hospitals in St Helens.

It used to be a fever hospital, or so she told us, so children often stayed there for a long time, and a song had grown up around their stay. Mother would sing it to us often as children, and as she became more locked into the past and less able to converse, she would it trot out frequently through the day.

Her version may not have been completely accurate but she always sang:

> I'm tired of Peasley Cross
> I want to go home,
> It's days and days and weeks and weeks
> since I had my tea at home.
>
> Mother, mother, take me home,
> from this convalescent home.
> I've been here a week or two,
> and now I want to be with you.
>
> So it's goodbye sanatorium,
> goodbye nurses too,
> Goodbye all the children,
> and Peter of the Ambulance too.

So my brother, who became 'Peter of the Ambulance', was despatched to look at a few homes close to his home in Wales, to see what he could find.

Jill, who also lived in Wales, recommended the one where her father had been several times on respite care while she was away on her adventures. It was in a large old house which overlooked a riding centre, so it sounded as if that would be rather nice for animal-loving Mother to be able to look out of the windows and see horses going past.

I knew the place as I'd competed at the adjacent riding centre many times when I was show jumping. I also knew Jill's father had a number of health issues, so felt there was a good chance that the level of care might fit Mother's needs.

My brother went to check it out and pronounced it too dark and gloomy inside. Instead he favoured a modern, purpose built home which provided full nursing care and seemed, he said, nice and clean and efficient. So shortly before I moved down to Wales, I packed up all of Mother's possessions from the home and said a sad goodbye to the staff. Mother was loaded into an ambulance direct from the hospital where she was still a patient, and made the long road trip down to South Wales.

My house was now empty. The tenant was safely installed. It was time for me and Meic to make our way down to my brother's house and begin the next leg of fox, chicken, corn, river.

I had held a faint hope that my brother might just have made some sort of effort with the total chaos in which he normally lived to prepare for my impending arrival.

When I reached the front door and found junk strewn all over the floor such that Meic and I could barely pick our way across, I headed up to the bedroom which was to be mine for the time being, sat down on the bed, put my arms around big, solid, cuddly Meic and howled and howled for the loss of my beloved little cottage.

But, onward and upward. Foxes and chickens and corn to be moved, rivers to be crossed, and next day, furniture to be taken up to the off road storage place in Hereford where my brother's bus was parked.

Travelling anywhere by road with my brother is always an experience, to put it mildly. He avoids motorways like the plague and always takes the scenic route, though it often doubles journey time. And he likes to make stopovers for the night on journeys which to other people would be an afternoon's journey there and back at the most.

So for the round trip from his home to Hereford, which according to Via Michelin is a journey of some two hours and eighteen minutes, we made not one but two overnight stopovers. I didn't mind too much since I love camping out, so did Meic. But it did seem a little excessive. Although, as it happened, very useful.

Our first stop was near Brecon. As we would be leaving the furniture van in storage on this occasion, I was following behind it in my brother's old Mercedes estate. I'd noticed how alarmingly the van was starting to wallow and roll on the journey and was only thankful there was no high wind.

As soon as we pulled into the camp-site car park and I parked next to the near side of the van, I could clearly see that the load had shifted to such an extent that the outer wall of the van was bowing outwards and an alarming crack had appeared in the corner of the bodywork.

I'm quite small and not very bulky, so I drew the short straw of climbing inside and burrowing my way through the precarious load to the far front corner, armed with rope to lash to the side bars of the van on the bowed side, pull as hard as my feeble frame allowed, and secure it to the bars of the opposite side.

I managed that reasonably well. The return journey to get out of the van proved rather more problematical. At one point I found myself well and truly wedged somewhere in the middle, with visions of having to be put into storage with the rest of the load.

Extricating myself involved twisting my left leg round at a angle at which it was never designed to be placed and half slithering, half climbing down the back of the load into a fairly undignified heap on the floor.

My brother was planning to sleep in the Luton of the van whilst Meic and I used our trusty tent. The camp-site didn't allow cars on the pitches and I was allocated a pitch a long walk from the car park, although the owner did come with a little golf buggy to help carry my things across. All a bit of a faff when you consider by this time we were barely 40 miles from our destination.

But no doubt my brother was in need of topping up his alcohol levels before we went any further and since he did at least have the sense not to drink then continue to drive, I was quite happy for a little break and to give Meic his favourite treat, a night in a tent, which we both thoroughly enjoyed as always.

So the next day we continued to trundle on our very slow way to the off-road storage to leave the lorry and camp another night in the field next to the village pub which my brother liked to frequent on his trips up there to play with his bus.

Once again he slept in the van whilst Meic and I were under canvas. Well, rip-stop nylon, strictly speaking, one of Millets finest.

That night we had the most incredible storm, with winds of such ferocity they managed to twist and break the carbon fibre pole of the tent's porch although, luckily, the main body of the tent stayed dry and weatherproof and Meic and I were able to get some sleep amidst the noise of the howling wind.

An aside here about going camping with a dog which suffers from psycho-motor seizures – if you're not interested in dogs, look away now. I understand why dogs make such first-rate medical alerts for all sorts of conditions as Meic always knew, about twenty minutes before their onset, that he was about to have one of his seizures.

His normally beautiful golden-brown eyes – I always said they looked like the colour of golden syrup at the bottom of the tin when it's settled – would change completely and go rather muddy looking and he would start to get agitated. Then with each rogue pulse that shot through his brain, he would be propelled forward, often with a loud yelp, and his jaws would snap uncontrollably on anything that was in the way.

Unlike with classic tonic-clonic epileptic seizures, which can be very violent but often of relatively short duration, Meic's psycho-motor seizures could last a long time – his worst was thirty six hours. It's sometimes called fly biting or fly catching syndrome as the dog does appear to be snapping at flies only he can see.

It's not the easiest of behaviours to manage in the small confines of a tent. My usual way of dealing with it, since medication had not stopped its occurrence and had had other side effects I didn't like, was simply to put Meic into a small-ish space of safety and leave him to it. If it happened when we were camping, I put him in the car while I went back to sleep in the tent.

Mercifully, with the storm and everything else to contend with, Meic had a quiet night and we both enjoyed our little adventure before heading back to Wales.

So now the fox, the chicken, the corn and the boat were all in the same principality. Phase one of the move had been accomplished.

Within three weeks, we were looking at different homes for Mother. Within four weeks I'd had enough and moved out of my brother's house, begging asylum from that best of best friends Jill, who lived nearby.

* * *

It's a sad fact of life that when things start out badly, they have a tendency to get worse rather than better. Within the first couple of visits to the nursing home, I knew it was not going to be all plain sailing.

One of the first incidents that made me realise how choppy the waters would be was over the unpacking of Mother's clothes.

I'd been in charge of her wardrobe for several years by this time. Mother loved shopping for bargains at charity shops and jumble sales. Living in Cheshire, there were some incredible finds to be made, very good labels at ridiculous prices. So as long as she was able to, I took her out rummaging round the charity shops. And when she could no longer go herself, I'd shop for her and bring her things I knew she'd like. So it's fair to say I knew every item of clothing she possessed.

I'd also personally checked everything was labelled with her name and had packed her cases myself for her move from Merseyside to Wales.

About the second time I visited her at the nursing home in Wales, just after she'd moved in, I'd found her a little something to wear so went to hang it up in the wardrobe in her bedroom and was very puzzled to find a number of items of clothing there which I knew were not hers. What's more, they were not remotely her size. Mother was small and slight, by this time barely over five foot and a size twelve in most things, with the occasional fourteen, just for a little extra comfort room.

Some of the horrors hanging there were size twenty-two. Mother has never been a size twenty-two in her life. Worse, Mother was particular about the quality and fabric of what she wore. Her own clothes were Chanel, Jaeger and similar, made from cotton, silk, linen and cashmere. These were more of the polyester and crimplene Bonmarché variety.

And whether or not you believe that people have a personal colour aura, you wouldn't need to spend long in Mother's company to know that she was ashes of roses and sage, lavender and beige. These were black, menopausal purple and bright red.

I went off to find the senior nurse on duty and explained, politely, that there had been a mix-up. She immediately assured me those were Mother's clothes, they were what had come with her and she herself had put Mother's name in them all.

I was tempted to ask her to put Mother into the bright purple crimplene track suit – we would have had to send in a search party to find her inside its voluminous size twenty-two folds.

Still politely, I pointed out all of the above factors, notably that I had personally name-labelled and packed all of Mother's clothes before she left Merseyside so that, whoever the clothes belonged to, it was certainly not her.

I wished I'd had the presence of mind to invite her to repack the contents of the wardrobe into the two small cases Mother had come with. The bright red overcoat alone would have completely filled one of them.

I was annoyed that I was not listened to and believed. I was annoyed they had not noticed what size my mother was and at least asked before labelling everything. I was annoyed because it showed a certain "we know best and you don't know anything about your mother" attitude I did not like. I gritted my teeth and thought it might get better.

It didn't.

We began to wonder if we had made a mistake in the choice of home in light of this attitude. We started looking around at what else there was in the area and found an absolutely beautiful one, with park-like grounds and a spectacular view of the Towy valley. But again, we would be up against the fact that it was a care home, not a nursing home, and as such might not be up to the level of care Mother needed.

Meanwhile, for me, sharing a house with my brother was proving to be far harder than I ever imagined it would be.

The house was theoretically large enough for us mainly to avoid one another. The layout was truly extraordinary, with its seven flights of stairs. Dinner guests had been known to leave the table to go to the bathroom and spend futile minutes afterwards going up and down staircases trying to find their way back to the room they had come from.

I was using a bedroom and a sort of study at the top, below the attic, to one side of the house, and we were sharing the kitchen. But everywhere was in such a depressing state of filth, squalor and chaos that even getting from bedroom to loo and back was arduous and potentially dangerous.

Many of the staircases had no bannisters. Electrical wires trailed everywhere – goodness knows which were live and which damaged. I did what I could to make it at least habitable, never mind preparing it for sale. I washed, scrubbed, disinfected and polished everything I could reach. I spent hours on my knees scraping up spilled plaster on the staircases and in the bathroom. And hours more hacking back the garden so it was at least possible to see the potential.

My brother continued to drink. I had tried on several occasions to help him by pointing him in the direction of professional help, as it was clear he was not capable of helping himself and I had neither the skills nor, to be frank, the patience to help him myself.

On one occasion when we were both at Mother's house preparing it for sale and he was yet again in a pathetic state of drunken weeping and saying he wanted to be made better, I made him an appointment at the nearby Priory Hospital, physically buttoned him into a clean shirt, drove him there and left him.

He lasted less then thirty six hours before saying they were all a bunch of wankers who didn't know what they were doing and discharging himself straight to the nearest pub.

I was lucky enough to have a friend who was an alcohol and addiction counsellor, who put me in touch with friends of hers who ran a rehab place in Lancashire, equally as good though not so well known, who said they would be delighted to help.

I arranged an interview for him. He went to the interview, announced that they were all wankers who wanted him to surrender his mobile phone and laptop and he couldn't possibly because of all the very important things he had to do, and refused to stay.

One memorable evening, after I moved into his house, he decided he simply had to watch the television in my bedroom, as it was the only one in the house working. He became verbally abusive and violent when I objected because I wanted to go to bed, so I said I'd had enough. The whole deal was off, I would go and stay with Jill and we'd have to rethink the whole project as I couldn't subject myself to that kind of abuse.

I arranged with Jill that I would go to her house the following day – it's in circumstances like these you find out who your true friends really are – but as at this point I didn't have a car, I was going to go on the train and Jill would meet me at the station.

By the following morning, as so often happens with alcoholics, my brother was much calmer and more sober and had either forgotten about the night before or had thought I was just having a temporary hissy fit which would all be in the past come the morning. He was so busy showing how very reasonable he could be and how hysterical I was being, he even drove me to the station.

I stayed with Jill for six days of blissful R&R to unwind and get my head straight, to see what could be salvaged from such a very messy state of affairs. Above all, I was trying to think what to do for Mother's best interests, having come so far in what was, largely, a venture to get her a better quality of life for whatever time she had left.

Time with Jill is always therapeutic. She knows when to talk and when to be silent. I tried to show my gratitude by ironing anything that wasn't tied down, since ironing is the only household chore I actually enjoy doing.

Whilst staying there, I walked down to the nearby garage where she bought her vehicles and had them serviced and repaired and did a deal with the owner for his own runabout van, an old blue Vauxhall Combo, complete with funky, flashing, orange light-bar.

I knew I would feel a lot happier and more secure with the independence of my own vehicle once again, rather than having to rely on borrowing my brother's old Mercedes, my own Golf having given up the ghost shortly before I moved in with my brother.

I was starting to feel, for Mother's sake, that I somehow had to pull the venture back from the brink and make the move happen. Back in more optimistic mode, I began thinking that with the independence of my own vehicle again I might just manage to make life tolerable. I knew it would also be sobering to my brother to know I could just walk out and drive off any time I wanted to.

I'd already showed him by my absence, by now six days, that I was quite capable of walking out if his behaviour became intolerable, which had shocked him rigid. If he felt I might just up sticks and go for good, perhaps he might just learn to control his behaviour towards me to an acceptable level.

I'd also noticed from the visitors' book and from talking to the staff that he hadn't once been to visit Mother in the six days I'd been away, although I had been visiting her daily. The amazing Jill had arranged insurance on her Suzuki 4x4 for me to drive whilst I was staying with her, before I bought the van. My brother and I had previously both been going every day, often separately, to give Mother as much company as possible, and to keep an eye on her.

*Even though mother was in a nursing home, I still visited every day and took her extra tea and fruit drinks to help avoid dehydration.*

Time to go back and find out what horrors awaited me.

When I got back and let myself in – no mean feat since security was quite an issue with my brother, although goodness knows why; no self-respecting burglar would dream of setting foot in a place which was in such total disarray and presented such an 'Elf and Safety risk to life and limb - my brother was sprawled out totally comatose on his bed with the door wide open. In other words, waiting to be found.

He was face down, so not in danger of choking on his own vomit. I spoke. I shouted. I banged on the door. He didn't stir. Kind and caring sister that I am, I took Meic out for the longest walk his dicky ticker and old legs could tolerate.

We slipped back into the same old rut, me trying to make some inroads in getting the place at least clean and tidy enough to show to prospective viewers, if nothing else. We made some progress in that I finally persuaded my brother to hire a succession of skips to start getting rid of some of the stuff that even he couldn't imagine would ever be of any further use.

One of the big problems in trying to clear any living space my brother inhabited was newspapers. You were simply not allowed to throw any of them away. Ever. His answer was always that there was some article in there that one day he might be going to read. And this had been going on for nearly thirty years, since the break-up of his marriage, when he'd stayed on in the marital home.

Things improved a little in that, as more holes started to appear in the management of our mother in the nursing home, we drew closer and were united in trying to fight her corner for her.

After several weeks, we noticed that she was never wearing her hearing aid. It's an easy thing to overlook when getting old ladies dressed and ready, but it did make life very difficult for us trying to talk to her, as without it she really was very deaf and that gave the impression that she was battier than she was. She'd actually been in the home seven weeks before I found the hearing aid, still unpacked, in one of her toilet bags.

We were neither pleased nor reassured, since her discharge care plan from the previous home quite clearly stated that she was deaf, wore a hearing aid, and needed to have the sub-titles on when watching television, as she was still capable of grasping some of what was going on by reading them. I personally put the hearing aid into the hand of the senior nurse on duty.

She put it in Mother's ear, checking with me that the fit was correct and it was in the correct ear. Two days later it was missing again and we were back to having shouted conversations, with Mother getting hold of completely the wrong end of the stick.

Mother had vascular dementia, not Alzheimer's disease. It's amazing, and alarming, how many people, including health care professionals, always assume it's the big A whenever anyone mentions dementia. Mother's short-term memory was completely gone in many areas. If you told her what day it was then asked her again five minutes later, she would have no clue.

But she knew who she was, who I was, who Meic was and who my brother was. She knew a lot about herself and delighted in telling people about going to the royal garden party and meeting the queen when the AP was president of the Guide of British Newspaper Editors.

She remembered the names of all her brothers and sisters though couldn't remember which ones were alive and which dead. Except for little Florrie. Because she'd died a long time ago, and Mother's long-term memory was still very good, hence remembering childhood poems. And she very rarely talked complete nonsense.

So when I arrived one day and Mother told me there was a lamb up a tree in the garden and she was worried about it because the weather wasn't very good and it had been there a long time without moving, I knew things were not well.

Off to the nursing station to find the senior nurse on duty and voice the concern that Mother might be dehydrated or starting a UTI, since those were the only occasions she was prone to hallucinating. I was assured she couldn't be dehydrated since she had eaten her tea.

Right.

The next day she was still the same, if a little more confused. The lamb hadn't moved at all, she was worried it may have been there all night and it wasn't right, leaving a poor lamb up a tree.

This time I spoke to two different senior nurses and was again told everything was fine. Because of course I couldn't possibly know my mother better than they did, having had her there all of seven weeks.

I was invited to Jill's for supper that night and was to stay on for the next week to babysit her collection of cats whilst she went on her half-term jaunt. It was no great surprise when I got a phone call on my mobile from the home to say that Mother had been taken to the nearby hospital.

I phoned my brother to update him and to tell him that I was on my way to pick him up and take him to the hospital. He wasn't even capable of taking my call, his one friend was round there and answered and relayed information between us.

My brother had obviously been drinking, heavily, probably from the moment I'd said I was going away for another week. As much as he disliked my presence in his life, he dislikes even more being alone.

He was no earthly use to man nor beast when I collected him, but I took him with me to the hospital where he promptly lurched off to find the canteen to get something to eat.

I spoke to a pleasant young A&E doctor, and voiced my earlier concerns about possible dehydration, with which she agreed. She put Mother on a drip and told me to encourage her to drink as much water as she could. Like me, she also seemed surprised that a nursing home hadn't been able to see dehydration coming on, or at least to have done something about it when it struck.

A litre or so of water later, she was back to what passed for normal – lots of "The Witch" and "Snowdrops", several "Mother, Mother it's a bugger"s, and no more about lambs up trees.

It was a pattern which was to repeat itself a few times. I would notice early warning signs that all was not well, report them to the senior nurse in charge, only to be fobbed off with increasingly bizarre stories. The one which perhaps most beggared belief was when I found Mother flushed and confused and with much redder lips than normal. I was told it was probably because she'd had jam for tea.

She had such a disturbed night that night that she managed to fall out of bed, so the doctor was called the following morning. He diagnosed oral thrush, a not uncommon side effect of dehydration in elderly patients. And so it went on.

My brother, in the meantime, was making trips to and from France trying, in his somewhat inept way, to bring the house purchase there to a conclusion so we could finally get Mother away from the home to where I would be able to take over most of her daily care. Most, because I knew I would need help getting her in and out of bed, since various episodes with horses had given me a few dodgy discs in my back and neck.

Then a very unexpected spanner fell into the works in the shape of me being ill. It's dangerous to say, but I am almost never ill. I don't do ill.

My brother was in France and texting me details of his journey back, saying he wanted me to drive to Cardiff to collect him. I'd had a nagging pain in my abdomen all day, rather like a bad case of trapped wind, and sent a text back to say I didn't really feel up to driving that distance, he would have to get a train back as far as his home town and I'd collect him from there, which I did.

I had another half-day of feeling not very well, followed by half a day of feeling quite unwell and spending most of the time in bed, apart from walking Meic, which was not easy as I had to go down three flights of stairs to get to the front door and was by now having some difficulty in standing upright.

I started to voice my concerns to my brother that I did appear to have quite a few of the symptoms of an acute appendicitis. As well as all his other problems, he is by way of being a professional hypochondriac who is always convinced his ailments are far worse than anyone else's. He pooh-poohed the suggestion, assuring me he'd often had something similar and it was just indigestion.

I was never especially close to my father but I did have some sympathy for him at the end of his life as he lay in his bed, wasted away to yellow skin and bone and quite clearly very close to death from cancer of the pancreas, having to endure my brother standing beside his bed giving him chapter and verse of how bad HE felt.

The next day I admitted defeat and went to the doctor. By this time I really could barely stand upright. The moment she saw me stagger into her surgery bent almost double she said: "Oh dear, I think it may well be your appendix, if you still have it."

I did. I was starting to wish I didn't. She gave a few gentle prods, which nearly made me leap through the ceiling, then pronounced she was convinced it was an acute appendicitis and she was going to phone and book me a bed direct on a ward rather than waste time sending me to A&E.

Do not pass go. Throw six to start again.

My brother had to drive me to the hospital, as by this time as I was doubled up to such an extent I couldn't see over the steering wheel. I was absolutely terrified, not for me but for the fact that the only thing I could do in the circumstances was to leave my beloved Meic in the very dubious care of my brother.

I set about writing out a careful list of his medication requirements for his heart condition and arthritis, his dietary needs, what exercise he needed and the required commands to make him relieve himself to order, which he was very good at doing.

I was still thinking I might be making a fuss about nothing, it was just trapped wind and if I could just manage one gargantuan fart, all would be well. I started to suspect it might actually be quite serious when, after examining me and asking for a scan, the duty registrar, seeing the nurse go for a wheelchair said: "Oh no, not in a chair, get someone to take her in the bed."

I'm rubbish at those questions when they say: "On a scale of one to ten how bad is the pain?" I don't know if it's my phobia of numbers or my brain is too analytical or what, but I can never come up with a quick, definitive answer. I kept assuring them that if I stayed very still and didn't move at all, and above all no-one poked me and said: "Does this hurt?", the pain barely registered on the scale. But when they did poke and prod me it probably climbed up above a five.

They kept asking me if it wasn't much more than that, and if I'd been sick at all. No, I hadn't been sick. I'm almost never sick. I probably hadn't been sick in more than thirty years and the last time might well have been the result of an over-indulgence of champagne.

I didn't want to make a fuss. I agreed with the nurse, I'd be fine in a chair, I certainly didn't want to be wheeled about in a bed like an ill person. I went for the scan.

When the consultant got the results, he said they were going to operate to remove my appendix. When? I asked. Immediately, he replied, it's just on the point of bursting. Oh. Not trapped wind then.

It was the first major surgery I'd ever had. In fact, only the second time I'd been in hospital, the first being when I had all four impacted wisdom teeth extracted under general anaesthetic. And yes, I've heard all the wisecracks about the lack of wisdom, believe me!

I don't know about this so-called curse on our family. I do know the consultant decided to let the baby registrar have his first-ever go at wielding a scalpel and let him loose on a full open procedure on me, none of this airy-fairy keyhole stuff.

So I woke up later that evening with a raging thirst and a very painful four-inch incision right across the major abdominal muscles, which has caused French doctors since to ask if, in Wales, they have very big knives, or very small spectacles, and whether Welsh surgeons actually know where an appendix is situated.

As soon as I was fully awake, I sent a text to find out how Meic, my darling boy, as I always called him, was doing, and whether he'd had his medication. Mercifully, he was the easiest dog to medicate of any I'd ever met. You just held out his pills, said "take your tablets", and he swallowed them with no fuss.

Unlike one of Jill's cats, Flip, whom I'd had to medicate daily whilst staying there to babysit the cats. Flip only had about one tooth in his head. He still managed to stick it into my thumb every time I tried to put his pill into his mouth.

When I finally succeeded in getting it into his mouth and preventing him from spitting it back out before he swallowed it, he gave me a thoughtful look and disappeared into the utility room. I was not totally surprised to hear noises off of cat vomiting. I was quite amazed at the skill of his aim in puking only into my pair of boots, missing all of Jill's footwear, which was close by.

My brother's reply was all about his woes, and wanting to check Meic's feeding arrangements, despite the very detailed written instructions I'd left. It wasn't very reassuring. He didn't ask how I was and I had to text again for a proper answer as to how Meic was.

I was determined to get out of hospital as quickly as I possibly could to get back to my boy. The morning after surgery, with a little encouragement from the charge nurse on duty, I was up, showered and dressed and sitting in my bedside chair when the consultant came on his rounds.

He looked surprised and asked how I was feeling. "Absolutely fine," I beamed brightly. He gave me an old-fashioned look and said: "Get up on the bed so I can examine you and I'll tell you how fine you are."

He had a poke and a prod – I was determined not even to wince – and gave me a long lecture on how appendicitis at my age was rare and serious, how I'd had major abdominal surgery and how I would have to stay at least a couple more days. Not very reassuring.

It was less reassuring later that day when my brother lurched in to see me, looking considerably the worse for wear. I was worried sick that he had sole custody of my boy and was driving around with him in the car when he was clearly in no fit state.

Jill had very kindly immediately sent a text, hearing where I was, offering to have Meic to stay with her. But a big boisterous collie in a house of elderly cats was not the best situation.

My brother had Meic in the car with him and although I was dying to see him and get a big, warm, furry hug and a kiss, there was no way I could make it down to the car park under my own steam, even for Meic, and no way my brother looked in any fit state to wheel me there, nor would have I trusted him to do so.

I decided to make a more determined break for freedom the next day, so was once again up, showered and sitting in a chair on morning rounds. But before that, I went to the day room and phoned my brother to see how Meic was. My brother sounded in a very bad way. According to him, he'd tripped over Meic's lead and fallen down several flights of stairs, banging his head.

He said he was concussed. He sounded concussed all right. Concussed as a newt. I had to ask several times how Meic was before I got a response to say he was fine. I didn't know whether or not I could believe him.

The young registrar was doing rounds that morning and when he came to my bedside, all the stress and worry of the last few days rather caught up with me. When he asked me how I was feeling, I burst into floods of tears and made an ET-like appeal to go home.

He was already apologetic about the state of the wobbly incision he'd left me with and this display of emotion was clearly a bit difficult for him to deal with. He said he'd have to ask a consultant about whether or not I could be discharged.

Thank goodness for a busy NHS system and Friday afternoons. It was a different consultant who came round later and he was clearly Mr "Clear 'Em All Out Before the Weekend". I explained I was worried sick about my precious dog in the hands of an alcoholic.

He examined me again and said he was perfectly happy that I was sane enough and sensible enough to seek medical advice at the least sign of anything like complications and that on that basis, he'd prescribe me some pain relief and sign my discharge form.

A quick text to Jill and she was on her way to pick me up and asked if, once I'd collected Meic, I wanted to go and stay with her for a few days until I was back on my feet. Have I mentioned that she is possibly the best best friend anyone could have?

When we got back to my brother's house, the front door of which opened directly onto a busy main road, I was very alarmed to see the door standing ajar, thinking of my boy. When we got into the ground floor room, a former shop converted into a sitting room, my brother was slumped in an armchair, barely conscious. But he did at least have Meic on a lead, the end of which was very thoroughly lashed to his wrist with one of his sailor's knots.

It's debatable which of us, me or Meic, was more pleased to see the other. A hug and a lick did wonders in making me feel better. Jill was all for taking me straight back to her place but seeing the state my brother was in, I thought I'd better stay.

Was there a welcoming pan of something tasty simmering on the stove for me? A kettle on the boil for a cup of tea? In your dreams. At one point my brother did open his eyes and say he had been having problems with the telephone, which probably meant that one of the extension phones somewhere in the house was off its hook. And that meant more than twelve rooms, including the large outhouse and outdoor conservatory, to check. Could I, he asked, just run up the stairs and start checking them.

Run? I asked him. I could still barely stand upright. I'd just had major abdominal surgery performed by a complete beginner armed only with the Young Surgeon's Guide to the Human Anatomy and a penknife, with the page on the appendix presumably missing. It would, and later did, take me ten minutes or more, to lumber up the stairs to my bedroom.

Welcome home.

* * *

The purchase of the pink house continued to rumble along. Deadlines came and went as my brother's chaotic lifestyle made it almost impossible for him ever to lay hands on the one vital document he needed at any particular moment.

We were at least starting to have some viewings of his property but, with me now laid up and unable to do any kind of manual work, certainly not what was needed to make that place presentable, the few brave viewers who came quickly beat a hasty retreat and probably dined out for weeks on the horror stories they told.

Finally, around the middle of December, my brother went back to France to do whatever it took to pull things together and conclude the deal.

And, after many agonising months, on the third of January, 2007, he signed the contract. The pink house was his. Time for the next round of fox, chicken, corn, river.

*It was both exciting and tantalising to think that Mother could soon be sitting on the warm south-facing patio of the "pink house"*

# Part Six:
# What Now

We'd bought, or at least my brother had, the pink house. There were a few things still to be sorted before we could move in, however. Most important was a telephone, as there currently wasn't one.

Although I was going to be caring for Mother more or less full-time, I needed some means to make a few pounds so I could start paying into the French system to qualify for health care, so much better than that which we'd experienced to date in the UK, although costly. Luckily my job was perfectly possible any-where I had an internet connection. But it needed to be a reliable one.

As my brother had still not yet sold his house in Wales, he was going to have to spend quite a bit of his time there sorting it out and packing it up. Which left me alone at the pink house with Mother. So clearly a phone-line was going to be doubly essential.

We also needed to put feelers out for some home carers to come morning and evening to get Mother out of bed and put her back into it. I had some neck problems after what I believe is called a Glasgow kiss from a horse called George. George flung back his head just as I was leaning forward, the top of his skull connected with my forehead and whip-lashed my head back with such force I heard lots of nasty crunching and tearing noises.

I was about an hour's ride from my riding centre in Wales at the time, with a group of customers I was bringing back from a day ride, and didn't dare dismount to check for damage for fear of not being about to get back on. This was long before the days of mobile phones and we were miles from anywhere, so the best bet was to ride gently home and see what was what.

It didn't really seem too bad. Until the following morning, when the only way I could get out of bed was by literally pulling my head up off the pillow by the hair, rolling off the bed onto my knees and hauling myself up using the door frame. Time for a visit to Accident & Emergency at the local hospital.

One of the people I had helping me at my riding centre around then was luckily able to drive so drove me down there. After a brief examination, I was sent for an X-ray then told to lie very still while it was studied as they thought I may possibly have broken a bone or slipped a disc and any movement could be very dangerous. Nice.

I lay there for quite some time, studying the not very clean ceiling. Then a fire alarm started to go off. Nobody came near me. I was balancing in my mind the choice between death by smoke inhalation or possible paralysis when my groom Judy appeared, drinking a cup of hot chocolate and completely unconcerned. It was, she told me, just a fire drill. Thanks for letting those of us lying like lemons in cubicles, waiting to be seen, know that essential piece of information.

George had done a pretty good job but had stopped short of anything major. I had a chipped vertebra, some torn ligaments, pulled muscles and strained tendons. Thanks, George. I was put in a very fetching neck collar, given pain killing pills so large I wondered if I was supposed to swallow them or stick them up

George's backside in revenge, and told to report back to fracture clinic in two weeks.

A physio told me much later I should have had a different shaped collar and been prescribed physiotherapy immediately. I didn't and I wasn't, with the result that the neck continued to give me trouble for ever more. Manhandling even Mother's slight weight too often was not an option.

We also needed to work out exactly how we were physically going to transport Mother without putting her health at risk. I initially favoured flying her out by specially equipped air ambulance with trained medics on board, which could have been done easily from the small air field not far from my brother's house to Clermont-Ferrand's Aulnat airport.

Unlike the AP, my brother and me, Mother had loved her only two experiences of flying. She had never flown whilst the AP was alive. He hated it so much he wouldn't contemplate doing it, so the times they went to Luxembourg, where they spent their honeymoon, they travelled by rail and sea, as did the whole family when we all went together in 1963 for the one thousandth anniversary of the Grand Duchy.

My father died in November 1988, on the day before his birthday. When the first anniversary of his death, and his birthday, came around, Jill and I decided to whisk Mother away to Spain's Costa de la Luz for a bit of welcome sunshine and a complete change of scene, to avoid any bad memories. And because when I travelled with Jill I managed to fly, it would be Mother's first ever trip in a plane.

I reassured her that there was no reason to expect she wouldn't enjoy it. In fact, if she was like her mother, sisters and brothers, she would love it. Intrepid Auntie Ethel had flown several times. I think Mother was probably the only one of her family who hadn't.

My only slight reservation was that we were flying into Gibraltar and, having done that the year before, I knew that it was a bit of a hairy landing. It's such a tiny landing strip, squashed between the sea and a big lump of rock, that they had to close the road while planes were coming in to land and taking off again, and it was certainly not my favourite landing place.

As we were coming into land on my first-ever visit to the Rock, a flight attendant announced, in that strange, adenoidal voice they often have: "Ladies and gentleman, we will shortly be landing at Gibraltar. On landing, you may notice a slight change in the noise of the engine. This is perfectly normal and is no cause for concern."

Slight change?? As in tortured squealing of reverse thrust, strong smell of burning rubber, screaming of brakes and rattling of the plane hard enough to make the overhead lockers fly open and a rain of luggage fall down on the passengers' heads? Would hate to think what the safe braking margin is on that runway before a plane piles into the Rock but wouldn't mind betting it's more in inches than feet!

But Mother was thoroughly looking forward to the whole experience. Especially the shopping for new outfits and selecting what to wear. She'd never before been to Spain and was probably fearing lager louts, chip shops and bingo. But the south Atlantic coast, certainly in those days, was incredibly quiet, unspoiled and beautiful, with mile upon mile of empty beach, especially in November.

Jill and I had happened on an apartment in Zahara de los Atunes the year previously, quite by chance. I'd got the bug for trail riding on horseback when I'd been previously to Spain's Sierra Nevada with my brother's ex-wife Debs.

That had been a strange experience for us both.

We'd booked it as a trail riding holiday, spending a week exploring some of the most remote villages of Spain, high in the Alpujarra region, on horse-back, staying in mountain inns each night. In fact it turned into more of a walking tour, leading our trusty mounts beside us. As Debs was recovering from a broken toe, we would certainly not have booked it, had we known.

We couldn't even work out the need for so much walking. Both experienced horsemen, we knew there were often occasions when it was prudent and desirable to dismount and lead ones horse, especially in a group which might include novice riders.

But we couldn't understand why we were often made to get down and walk on perfectly safe-looking tracks which were quite flat and level, the horses were not tired, and it was not in the full heat of the day. It was only by one of life's bizarre coincidences I found out the truth a few years later when a customer at my riding centre turned out to have been on the same trail ride at another time.

She told us that on one occasion the guide was allowing some of the riders to go ahead – something I, as a trail leader, would never allow – and they were galloping on a little too strongly. One horse and rider had gone over the edge of a river canyon and both had been killed. Hence the caution.

Jill and I had become good friends when she started riding at my equestrian centre in Wales in the mid 1980s. Luckily she discovered quite early on that I'm completely mad and seemed able to deal with it.

With friends and regular customers, it was standard practice, after an enjoyable ride, to invite them into either the big kitchen or the converted barn dining room for tea and whatever home-made cakes or scones were on the menu.

We were a bit low on cakes that day, there was only one piece left, so wishing to make sure my two grooms didn't steal it whilst I was out on the ride with Jill, I very pointedly picked it up in front of them and licked it, so I knew it would be safe.

When we got back from a nice blow across the tops of the hills and moorland, we sat down to a cup of tea, and the one piece of cake was staring reproachfully at us from its place of honour. I could see that Jill was looking hungry and kept eyeing the cake, which was a particularly delicious looking Victoria sponge.

In the end I had to come clean and confess why I was not able to offer her a slice. It says a lot for her that we have remained friends ever since!

Jill had already done several trail rides in different countries and jumped at my suggestion that we should go together to Spain and do one there. I'd seen an advert and got some information on one, departing from Zahara de los Atunes, not far from Cape Trafalgar, and doing a loop round the hills behind the coastal land there. We decided to book it, and our flight to Gibraltar, where we were to be met by the person running the trail rides, a British ex-pat – let's call her Sonja.

Perhaps my brother's theory of a curse is not all that far-fetched after all. Just a few short days before we were due to go, I had a phone call from Sonja to say that because of an outbreak of deadly African horse sickness in the area, all her horses were quarantined and could not be ridden. If we still wished to go, she said, she would give us a discount off the price of the week's holiday, plus a free hire car for the week in lieu of riding.

We highly doubted that our holiday insurance would pay out on African horse sickness quarantine cancellation, and we were both in need of a break in the sun. So we decided to go anyway and just enjoy exploring the region by car rather than on horseback.

Sonja was, to say the least, a little on the eccentric side. And her driving was certainly an experience, and not one for the faint hearted. As she drove us, erratically, back to Zahara, she told us there was a choice of accommodation, either a room at an hotel or an apartment.

She took us first to the hotel and to the available room. An English couple, who were just finishing their week there and had not yet departed, were sitting in the room playing Trivial Pursuit. They told us how pleased they were to have brought the Trivial Pursuit with them as they'd spent many a happy hour up in their room playing it.

Jill and I didn't say anything but both exchanged a "there has to be more to life than this" sort of look.

We asked if we could possibly have a look at the apartment as well, just for comparison. The hotel room was clean and adequate, twin beds, sparsely furnished, as is the style in that part of Spain, and handy for the bar and restaurant downstairs. But nothing special.

Sonja drove us to the other side of town and appeared to have lost the plot completely as she drove onto the beach. But she then turned into the entrance of a building called La Colmena – the beehive. It was a very attractive white building, with archways everywhere and a beautiful garden, full of exotic palms and bougainvillea.

There was lots of Moorish mosaic tiling everywhere, particularly up the steps to the various apartments, including the one to which Sonja was taking us. Inside it was beautifully light and well appointed, with three bedrooms, an open airy living area, small but well equipped kitchen and a beautiful balcony overlooking the beach and the sea.

We played it cool and said it was all right, the hotel had been so very nice, but we were here now and it would inconvenience Sonja to have to drive us back to the hotel so we were happy to stay and slum it in the apartment. (Which was fabulous.)

Jill liked it so much that, after that first visit, she'd already been back there since with her mother before we booked it again to take my mother out. Mother loved every minute of the holiday, from fastening her seat belt for her first ever take off. She loved the flight. She was like a child, loving her fiddly in-flight meal for its novelty. She had great fun peering out of the window, even coming into land, and appeared completely unconcerned by the entire flying experience.

After that, I'd been very brave and taken her out to visit the family in Luxembourg by plane. Much as I hate flying, I have to confess that, with Mother's house less than six miles from Manchester airport, the convenience of having lunch with her then afternoon tea with the cousins in Luxembourg, after the short hop, made it almost worthwhile.

Until Mother and I were walking down the long, glass-lined corridor looking for the correct gate and our plane.

"Is that our plane?" Mother asked, and I looked out hopefully at a nice big, solid, shining plane that look well up to the short flight.

It was only then that I realised that the tiny little object crouching beside it, which was so small I'd taken it for the baggage truck, was actually the little Brasilia jet that was due to carry us.

I was utterly, heart-stoppingly, terrified for the entire flight. Mother sat up at the window, oohing and aahing in delight and enjoying the champagne, asparagus, fresh strawberries and cognac that went with the business class tickets.

So I was confident that she wouldn't find the flight out to France at all worrying. The advantage of it being a fairly short journey would balance the cost, which was not inconsiderable, and did include fully trained medical staff with her at all times.

My brother was not convinced. A true pessimist by nature, he kept saying what if something happened while she was up there and she needed to go to hospital. I pointed out that she could probably be landed and taken to hospital faster than if she was in a road vehicle. I think he was largely projecting his own fear of flying onto her.

I was just keen to get Mother out of that home as soon as humanly possible. There continued to be episodes which disturbed me, and a few in the run up to Christmas which caused us to make a formal complaint to the management.

Despite her dementia, Mother was still perfectly capable of saying what she liked and didn't like, especially when it came to food. She was not, and never had been, a fussy eater and was quite adventurous and willing to try new dishes.

But she had never liked dried fruit, in which I take after her. Not for her, or me, the mince pies, Christmas pud and Christmas cake traditions. We far preferred a nice light Pavlova, a fruit tartlet or a light, moist chocolate cake.

One afternoon when I was, as usual, sitting with her in the day room watching something mindless on television, probably Midsomer Murders, one of the carers came round with the afternoon tea tray and some mince pies.

We both said yes to cups of tea but no to mince pies. To my horror, the carer said how nice the mince pies were, picked one up and attempted to stuff it into Mother's mouth. I'm still not quite sure how I didn't hit her.

I was so angry I went straight to the manager's office and asked for an appointment to see her the next day. I explained I was so angry at that moment that I didn't trust myself to speak then.

The next day she professed horror at the incident, assured me it was totally out of character and the staff member in question would receive additional training.

Then Christmas Day itself was very bad. When I got there in the morning, with Mother's presents, the day room was, understandably, full of visiting relatives. And it being Wales, equally understandably, they were all speaking Welsh, together with the carers and staff who were mingling amongst them and handing out presents from under the tree to all of the residents.

Except Mother.

Mother was sitting all alone in the midst of this noise. She didn't speak any Welsh. Nobody was taking the slightest bit of notice of her. She had wet herself and was sitting in sodden trousers, looking very uncomfortable.

*Luckily long-suffering Meic was always on hand to help*
*cheer Mother up when needed, even being recruited*
*as Santa's little helper at Christmas time.*

When I got to her, she pointed to all the other residents busy unwrapping presents and said to me forlornly: "Aren't I getting a present?"

We have never been a touchy-feely, huggy family but at that moment I just wanted to throw my arms round her, give her a big hug and tell her that everything was going to be all right.

At that moment her designated carer appeared, a nice enough woman, and utterly mortified. Designated carers personally see to buying presents for "their" residents, which are then wrapped and put under the tree with a label with each recipient's first name on. Despite working in the home for some fourteen years, this carer had failed to realise Mother was not the only Nell in the home, so someone else had got her present.

The carer had been to retrieve it and handed it over to Mother, hastily and clumsily re-wrapped after being opened in error. Quite a nice pink dressing gown. But a little late, the hurt had been caused.

I insisted Mother was immediately taken to be cleaned up and changed, put into clean new clothes and brought back, then spent a lot of time making a fuss of her and helping her to unwrap all the small gifts I'd brought for her, since I thought she would appreciate a lot of little gifts rather than one big one, which she appeared to do.

Although her verdict on the whole affair, just as I was leaving, was: "Mother, Mother, it's a bugger, sell the pig and buy me OUT," said with even more feeling than usual.

But seeing her sitting there so forlorn, like a little girl lost, had really affected me. I hated it when she was treated like an invisible nobody, just because she was old and losing her faculties.

And sad to say, it was an attitude which prevailed, even in a nursing home where the staff should have known better.

There was another occasion when I was sitting with Mother, talking and having a cup of tea, when the home manager marched up and without even a greeting, certainly not to Mother, stuck a ring in front of my face and said: "Is this your mother's ring?"

I was appalled by the lack of tact and good manners. I simply took the ring, passed it to Mother and asked her if it was hers. "No, I don't have one like that," she replied. "I don't know whose that is, I've never seen it before."

Perhaps what was more disturbing about that incident, and the attitude it illustrated, was when I later spoke to the manager and told her how very impolite I had found it to be, she simply said she'd assumed Mother wouldn't know and would want to claim the ring for herself.

\* \* \*

My brother had started on the job of moving our collective possessions out to the pink house. We had become quite friendly with the owner of the skip hire business we were using to at least start on the clearance of my brother's house. He was an ex-boxer who leapt at the suggestion that he should drive my brother and his furniture van out there with the first load of things.

It was to be his first experience of the Channel tunnel and he clearly had some difficulty in grasping the whole concept. My brother overheard him on his mobile to a friend during the drive down to Folkestone saying he was on his way to the bridge to France and would be arriving in Carlisle at the other side.

My brother had also finally definitely decided that, rather than spend a lot of money on airlifting Mother to France, he would prefer to buy a motorhome, complete with shower room and toilet, and transport her in that, with nursing staff in attendance. This would mean he would then have the motorhome as an asset afterwards and that, should Mother's health give cause for concern on the journey, it should be a fairly simple matter to divert to the nearest hospital for medical attention.

I continued to battle with the home about poor standards of care. Mother's hearing aid kept being missed off her morning dressing routine and it really did present difficulties trying to talk to her when she wasn't wearing it.

There was one occasion when we were trying to tell her some news of one of our Luxembourg cousins, Nadine (pronounced, in Luxembourg, as Nah-deen, with the emphasis on the second syllable, rather than the stress on the first syllable as sometimes is the case in English.)

Mother looked puzzled and asked: "The Dingley? What's the Dingley?", after which the motorhome which my brother bought for the journey always carried the nickname of The Dingley.

Thanks to the boy scout penknife efforts on my appendix, my scar was healing very slowly and at one point appeared to have a slight infection. So I was still not able to do very much, but did what I could to keep my brother's house clean and presentable, and to show it to a procession of would-be buyers.

Some said it was interesting. Some came back for second viewings, trailing others in their wake. But I think that was just to share the novelty of such a strange place. None of them showed any inclination to buy. In addition, the property market was starting a very significant down-slide, with prices falling and sales heading towards a standstill.

We were planning on a mid-March move to the pink house, hoping that we could all be safely installed there before the twenty-eighth of March, which would be Mother's ninetieth birthday.

My brother had found a motorhome online which he liked the look of, near his off-road storage in Hereford. We went up there, had a look and he decided to buy it. There was a long bench seat, which served as a single bed, down one side, and the table and seating area could be converted into a double bed. So if Mother was too tired to do the journey sitting upright, she could easily be put to bed.

We'd had a slight problem of late with her being travel sick. She frequently complained of back pain, because of the osteoporosis, and was on morphine patches for it, which tended to make her sickly. But with medical escorts, we felt this problem could probably be overcome.

Not all of the carers and nursing staff at the home where she was were bad. Two in particular were very good indeed, two Bulgarian ladies, who seemed a great deal more switched on than a lot of the other staff, including some of the senior nurses – especially those who mistook the symptoms of dehydration and oral thrush for the after effects of eating jam.

We booked one outside agency qualified nurse to escort Mother on the journey. She came to meet Mother and the two got on very well. She would travel with us to the pink house then return to the UK as soon as we arrived. But we thought it would be nice for Mother, and very helpful for me, if one of the people who had been looking after her for the past eight months or so could travel out with her and perhaps stay a day or two to help me get into the routine.

It has to be said I didn't really know what I was taking on. I hadn't even ever had a baby, nor looked after one. And suddenly I was going to be in sole charge of what was effectively a ninety-year-old baby, highly dependent and incontinent, though thankfully normally not doubly so.

So more in hope than anticipation, we put up an advert in the home for someone to travel out, spend a few days, including some time off, and enjoy an all-expenses paid trip home on the Eurostar, all at slightly more than normal care work rates.

We were absolutely thrilled when one of the Bulgarian carers, the best of all of them by far, said she would like to do it. She was so very competent we couldn't really understand why she was doing only a low-paid carer's job when she was clearly much more highly trained.

Once we got talking to her, we discovered she had trained and qualified as a nurse in Bulgaria and worked there as one. But she was no linguist and her English was not good enough to enable her to work as a nurse in the UK. It must have been so difficult for her to have to be under the supervision of people less qualified and less competent, but she was always very professional, and above all, always warm and caring towards Mother.

There were inevitably a few potential last-minute hitches.

It proved more difficult than anticipated to get Mother's passport renewed in good time. Clearly she could not make the journey to a passport office to apply in person so my brother would have to go and do so for her. But the telephone advice on what he needed to take was most unhelpful.

Mother had made an enduring power of attorney over all her affairs whilst she was still capable of doing so, naming me and my brother as joint attorneys. We explained this on the phone and were told it would be accepted – as long as Mother wrote and signed a letter explaining that she had made it and that the person carrying it was her attorney.

Er, the whole point of the power of attorney was that she was no longer capable of managing her own affairs. Had she been capable of writing such a letter, she would have been equally capable of applying for her own passport. As it was she was no longer capable of holding a pen most of the time, much less of signing anything very much.

Luckily a trip to her GP solved that problem. He was quite happy to write and sign a letter of explanation, confirming her identity and circumstances. And he didn't seem to think it was such an outrageous plan to try to take her to France. His attitude seemed to be, she's nearly ninety, with a not very positive prognosis. Why not give her the chance of one last adventure?

And so, on the morning of Monday, March the nineteenth, 2007, we left the nursing home for the last time in convoy, my brother driving The Dingley, with the nurse and the Bulgarian carer in the back with Mother, and me following behind with Meic in my little blue van which I'd named, with all the imagination and originality which makes me such a good copywriter, Blue.

It was a long old haul down to Folkestone. Even with facilities on board, they had to stop the motorhome a few times for Mother's travel sickness. But we made it and lined up in the queues ready to board the shuttle.

I was relying on following my brother. He had booked rooms at the Kyriad Hotel in Calais, one for Mother and the carers and one for himself, but I'd declared myself quite happy to sleep in The Dingley with Meic, not then realising that dogs are welcome almost anywhere in many parts of France, and certainly in many hotels. I didn't know the way to the hotel but was planning on following the motorhome.

As luck would have it, just as we were boarding, I was waved into a different lane altogether and found myself loaded into a different compartment. So much for my convoy theory. And my mobile phone couldn't find any signal to contact my brother.

By the time we arrived in France, it was quite dark. I decided to drive out of the terminal and see what I could find and was delighted at how quickly I found signs to the Kyriad Hotel.

Feeling full of triumph, I soon found it and swung into the car park. There was no sign of The Dingley, so I just assumed they had been unloaded after me, and Meic and I went for a much needed little leg-stretch around the car park and surrounding area.

There was still no sign of the motorhome. I was starting to flag a bit by this time. I went into reception and asked which rooms my brother had booked. The receptionist could find no record of any booking in our name.

But at least I now had a mobile signal, so I phoned my brother and asked him where he was. "At the Kyriad Hotel," he replied. "Well, I'm at the Kyriad Hotel," I replied, "I can't see any signs of you or the Dingley and the receptionist has never heard of you."

I went back into reception. Of course, there were two Kyriad Hotels in Calais. We were both at a different one. After a somewhat tiresome journey trying to find and follow signs to the other one, I arrived and caught up with the other weary travellers, who were planning an evening meal.

After such a long and difficult day I wasn't keen on leaving Meic alone in the van, especially in what was not a very salubrious area, to join them. But again I hadn't appreciated the difference in French and British culture towards dogs.

When we asked if a well-behaved dog would be allowed to join us at table, the waiter said but of course, as if it was the most natural thing in the world and didn't even need asking. Meic was thrilled, and settled himself quietly down at my feet, obviously very content with his first experience of being a French dog.

We were all very tired. But Mother was quite bright and enjoyed her supper and certainly didn't look any the worse for her journey so far. Although by the time her two carers took her off to put her to bed, I suspect she was as relieved as the rest of us finally to be putting her head on a pillow and stretching out to sleep.

The next day we all, Meic included, breakfasted at table together, and then it was time to head off on the final leg of our long journey. Most people take around seven hours from the channel ports to Clermont-Ferrand, and we were headed for a point about thirty miles north of there.

But my brother has an almost pathological hatred of motorways and goes to any lengths, literally, to avoid them, even if it adds miles to his journey. This is particularly true of Paris's infamous périphérique ring road. It can admittedly at times be a bottleneck to rival the M25. But if you hit it at the right time you can often sail through and on your way, cutting off valuable miles.

My brother's preferred route goes through Reims. If you don't know it, have a look on an atlas of France and see if it seems the logical route to you.

To be fair, he couldn't have known there would have been a road accident just there, causing us to be held up at one junction for a good hour. With the end result that our driving time finished up as more than thirteen hours.

And whereas driving the large motorhome with Mother in the back was probably quite tiring and stressful, he did at least have the company of the two carers, who could pass him food and drink and keep him awake.

I was on my own with Meic and, as the hours rolled by and we seemed no nearer to our destination, I really did start to wonder if I was making a monumental mistake.

Stop the world, I want to get off.

But then, suddenly, we were driving up the familiar steep hill and pulling into the driveway of the pink house. We had done it. We had arrived in France. All of us. The new adventure had begun.

Was it going to be a successful one? Had I done the right thing or would I soon be sending text messages to my friends saying: "Mother, Mother, it's a bugger, sell the pig and buy me OUT"?

## THE END

Made in the USA
Charleston, SC
14 February 2014